Building Your Business from Heaven Down 2.0

More Markers from the Business Complex of Heaven

by

Dr. Ron M. Horner

Building Your Business from Heaven Down 2.0

More Markers from the Business Complex of Heaven

By

Dr. Ron M. Horner

www.CourtsOfHeaven.Net
PO Box 2167
Albemarle, North Carolina 28002

Building Your Business from Heaven Down 2.0

More Markers from the Business Complex of Heaven

Copyright © 2020 Dr. Ron M. Horner

Scripture is taken from the New King James Version®. Copyright © 1982 by Thomas Nelson. Used by permission. All rights reserved. (Unless otherwise noted.)

Scripture quotations marked (Phillips) are taken from The New Testament in Modern English by J.B. Phillips copyright © 1960, 1972 J. B. Phillips. Administered by The Archbishops' Council of the Church of England. Used by Permission.

Scripture quotations marked (TPT) are from The Passion Translation®, Copyright © 2017, 2018 by BroadStreet Publishing Group, LLC. Used by permission. All rights reserved. ThePassionTranslation.com

Any trademarks mentioned are the property of their respective owners.

All rights reserved. This book is protected by the copyright laws of the United States of America. This book may not be copied or reprinted for commercial gain or profit. The use of short quotations or occasional page copying for personal or group study is permitted and encouraged. Permission will be granted upon request.

Requests for bulk sales discounts, editorial permissions, or other information should be addressed to:

LifeSpring Publishing
PO Box 2167
Albemarle, NC 28002 USA

Additional copies available at www.courtsofheaven.net

ISBN 13 TP: 978-1-71665-376-6
ISBN 13 eBook: 978-1-71665-373-5

Cover Design by Darian Horner Design (www.darianhorner.com)
Images: stock.adobe.com #: 202697770
123rf.com #: 29029456

First Edition: August 2020

10 9 8 7 6 5 4 3 2 1

Printed in the United States of America

Notice

The information in this book is not legal or financial advice. For your legal or financial situations, you should consult your legal or financial professional. No advice or information given should constitute "legal or financial advice," but rather you are encouraged to trust God for your overall business and financial advice. Use your personal cumulative wisdom in following the information presented in this book.

Disclaimer

The author, Dr. Ron M. Horner, is not an attorney or financial advisor or tax professional. The information herein is reflective of his personal and ministerial experience and should not be construed as professional legal or financial advice. Neither Dr. Ron M. Horner, or LifeSpring Publications are responsible for the use or misuse of this information.

Get the Declaration of Trade Guide FREE!

Simply follow this link and obtain the downloadable PDF of this valuable guide.

Visit:

https://dot.basglobalconsulting.com

Table of Contents

Acknowledgements i
Preface iii
Chapter 1 Wealth Creation 1
Chapter 2 Pulling Down Strongholds in Business 7
Chapter 3 The Declaration of Trade
 & Deed of Commerce & Trade 17
Chapter 4 The Primacy of Heaven 25
Chapter 5 First Fruits & Tithes 33
Chapter 6 Creative Downloads 43
Chapter 7 Mind Mapping with a Twist 47
Chapter 8 How to Work with Your Angel Part 1 53
Chapter 9 How to Work with Your Angel Part 2 65
Chapter 10 Capturing Your Dreams 87
Chapter 11 Questions & Answers 97
Chapter 12 Conclusion 103
Appendix A 105
Learning to Live Spirit First 105
Four Keys to Hearing God's Voice 113

Appendix B 115
Creating Your Declaration of Trade 115
Appendix C 117
Glossary 117
Business Advocate Services 123
Description 141
About the Author 143
Books by Dr. Ron M. Horner 145

Acknowledgements

Thanks goes to my wife Adina and youngest daughter Darian, and Donna Neeper, my gifted Executive Assistant, without whose assistance the obtaining of these revelations would have been far more challenging.

Also let me express my appreciation to my faithful team of co-laborers and intercessors and those who partner with LifeSpring International Ministries. Blessings to all of you.

Preface

Bible teacher Joyce Meyer wrote a book years ago, entitled *The Battlefield of the Mind*, which aptly describes where many people live their lives. They may never be able to step into a place of victorious living due to the dominance their soul has over their minds. We were not designed to live that way. We were built to live "spirit first." Your spirit is designed to interface with Heaven and instruct you from the realms of Heaven, yet many of us – nearly all of us – have yet to learn how to live spirit first. Rather, the soulish arena has dominated our lives, although it was never designed to do so.

> *[17] And take **the helmet of salvation**, and the sword of the Spirit, which is the word of God; [18] praying always with all prayer and supplication in the Spirit, being watchful to this end with all perseverance and supplication for all the saints— [19] and for me, that utterance may be given to me, that I may open my mouth boldly to make known the mystery of the gospel, [20] for which I am an ambassador in chains; that in it I may speak boldly, as I ought to speak. Ephesians 6:17 (Emphasis mine)*

The Passion Translation renders this verse in an even richer fashion:

> *¹⁷ Embrace the power of salvation's full deliverance, **like a helmet to protect your thoughts from lies**. And take the mighty razor-sharp Spirit-sword of the spoken Word of God. ¹⁸ Pray passionately in the Spirit, as you constantly intercede with every form of prayer at all times. Pray the blessings of God upon all his believers. ¹⁹ And pray also that God's revelation would be released through me every time I preach the wonderful mystery of the hope-filled gospel. Ephesians 6:17-19 (TPT) (Emphasis mine)*

Paul references the Helmet of Salvation in another passage that we often overlook.

> *⁸ But let us who are of the day be sober, putting on the breastplate of faith and love, and as **a helmet the hope of salvation**. ⁹ For God did not appoint us to wrath, but to obtain salvation through our Lord Jesus Christ, ¹⁰ who died for us, that whether we wake or sleep, we should live together with Him. 1 Thessalonians 5:8-10 (Emphasis mine)*

Again, The Passion Translation adds a richness to the translation:

> *⁸ But since we belong to the day, we must stay alert and clearheaded by placing the breastplate of faith and love over our hearts, **and a helmet of the hope of salvation over our thoughts.***

⁹ For God has not destined us to experience wrath but to possess salvation through our Lord Jesus, the Anointed One. ¹⁰ He gave his life for us so that we may share in resurrection life in union with him—whether we're awake or asleep.
1 Thessalonians 5:8-10 (TPT) (Emphasis mine)

You have a promise of protection!

The Helmet of Salvation is not merely an object, it is also a dimensional place of protection you can step into for your thoughts. Say this: "I step into the dimensional place of the Helmet of Salvation, in Jesus' name." You can live in a place where your thought life is protected 24/7.

Our challenge to this way of life comes because the soul is experiencing role confusion. It feels it should always protect us and determine what is valid or invalid. It wants to be in charge of your life, when the fallacy is that it was never designed for that role – your spirit, however, was designed to fill that role. Your soul has gained its information from the Tree of the Knowledge of Good and Evil, which is the wrong tree to eat from. Your spirit, on the other hand, wants to draw from the Tree of Life – the other tree that was in the Garden of Eden.

Paul describes how the spirit and soul should function in his first letter to the Corinthian believers in chapter 2, beginning in verse 6. Read it from The Passion Translation:

⁶ However, there is a wisdom that we continually speak of when we are among the spiritually mature. It's wisdom that didn't originate in this present age, nor did it come from the rulers of this age who are in the process of being dethroned. ⁷ Instead, we continually speak of this wonderful wisdom that comes from God, hidden before now in a mystery. It is his secret plan, destined before the ages, to bring us into glory. ⁸ None of the rulers of this present world order understood it, for if they had, they never would have crucified the Lord of shining glory. ⁹ This is why the Scriptures say: Things never discovered or heard of before, things beyond our ability to imagine—these are the many things God has in store for all his lovers. ¹⁰ But **God now unveils these profound realities to us by the Spirit. Yes, he has revealed to us his inmost heart and deepest mysteries through the Holy Spirit, who constantly explores all things.** ¹¹ *After all,* **who can really see into a person's heart and know his hidden impulses except for that person's spirit? So, it is with God. His thoughts and secrets are only fully understood by his Spirit, the Spirit of God.** ¹² *For we did not receive the spirit of this world system but the Spirit of God, so that we might come to understand and experience all that grace has lavished upon us.* ¹³ *And we articulate these realities with the words imparted to us by the Spirit and not with the words taught by human wisdom.* **We join Spirit-revealed truths with Spirit-revealed words.**

¹⁴ Someone living on an entirely human level rejects the revelations of God's Spirit, for they make no sense to him. He can't understand the revelations of the Spirit because they are only discovered by the illumination of the Spirit. ¹⁵ Those who live in the Spirit are able to carefully evaluate all things, and they are subject to the scrutiny of no one but God. ¹⁶ For Who has ever intimately known the mind of the Lord Yahweh well enough to become his counselor? Christ has, and we possess Christ's perceptions *(we have the mind of Christ)*. 1 Corinthians 2:6-16 (TPT) (Emphasis mine)

Live spirit first!

Are you willing to embrace change? Are you willing to embrace a different way of doing things? Of thinking? Of operating? If the answer is yes, then your quest will start with this simple instruction:

Fire the fear!

Fear is an expression of your soul which considers itself to be out of control in a situation. You must fire it and give it no more leadership in your life. You must begin to see yourself accessing Heaven and learn to flow in creativity's river from Heaven. Another definition of fear is **F**aith **E**mbracing an **A**lternate **R**eality. It is faith in the wrong thing, or faith working in the wrong direction. Fear need not be embraced on any level in your life. We need to allow the love of our Heavenly Father to conquer us so that fear can NEVER conquer us.[1]

As you read through this book, remember the instruction of Jesus that you must be childlike to access the Kingdom of Heaven. Children have a great degree of innocence and are not prone to pre-judge what they see, hear, or experience. Unfortunately, we as adults have spent a lifetime being experts at prejudging our experiences. If an experience does not fit in our nice, little, comfortable box, we dismiss it as invalid. I challenge you to take off your "adult suit" and put on your "kid suit" as you read this book. Begin to imagine again and simply believe that your Father genuinely loves you and has good things in store for His kids, of which you are one. You have permission to be child-like as you go through this book. You will be amazed at how free you will be to recharge your hopes and dreams.

Over the next few hours as you read this book, we want you to be mantled or covered in hope by putting on the hope of salvation (and all that it has provided for you) as a helmet. Pause right now to prophetically act out putting on a helmet, just like you would do if you were a child.

---

[1] Lord, even when your path takes me through the valley of deepest darkness, fear will never conquer me, for you already have! You remain close to me and lead me through it all the way. Your authority is my strength and my peace. The comfort of your love takes away my fear. I'll never be lonely, for you are near. Psalms 23:4 (TPT)

...the hope of salvation as a helmet.[2]

As you put your helmet on, realize that a helmet provides protection for your thoughts. When you feel protected, fear and worry are absent.

Protection gives you the ability to freely flow in creativity without fear, knowing that you are protected because you have on the salvation of the living Lord.

God can take care of you and help you guard your thoughts. Creativity cannot flow freely where you do not feel safe. The safest place to be is under the protection of the Father. To accomplish this, however, you need to speak to your soul and tell it to step back and relinquish control. Then, speak to your spirit and say, "Spirit, come forward. I relinquish control to you to obey Holy Spirit now." Notice the difference.

For some of you, your soul may have been reluctant to follow your instruction to back up, but you, via your will operating from your spirit, have the authority and right to instruct your soul in what to do. Your soul is supposed to be a servant to assist you in engaging the realms of Heaven. It is not intended to be your master, dictating what Heaven does in you, through you, or because of you. The passage of scripture you just read

---

[2] 1 Thessalonians 5:8

from in 1 Corinthians 2 reminds us that things from Heaven can only be received via your spirit. Your soul is not equipped for that type of engagement, but your spirit is fully equipped to engage the realms of Heaven.

Spirit come forward!

Living spirit first is a liberating lifestyle. If you have had a heart to follow the Lord in full obedience, this is the type of lifestyle the Apostle Paul was speaking of to all the believers and churches he wrote to. To the Colossians he instructed, "if you are risen with Christ, seek the things which are above and not the things of the earth.[3]" He continues by saying, "Set your mind on things above, not on things on the earth.[4]" To live without a cognizance of Heaven is to be short-changing your walk with God. **You are a spirit being first and foremost.** Your physical body and your soul will cease existing at some point, but your spirit is designed to be eternal. Additionally, we do not have to wait until our body ceases to function to experience the wonders and riches of Heaven. We can begin today!

Learn to live spirit first!

As you go through these chapters, focus on learning spirit first. Some things you will need to read and then

---

[3] Colossians 3:1

[4] Colossians 3:2

re-read, because you need to "catch" what Heaven is saying. Throughout the book, whenever you sense your soul trying to evaluate what you are reading, simply remind it of its position secondary to your spirit. You are choosing to live spirit first. You have been living soul first for decades, and chances are, that way of living has had its drawbacks. Your spirit is absolutely thrilled to be able to freely engage the realms of Heaven. It is designed for it and has been waiting your entire existence to begin this lifestyle through you. It has wanted your expression of living to be from Heaven down, where Heaven is first, not from earth upward. That is the real you. So, make the choice to live *Heaven down – Heaven first!*

The content of this book is essentially the information taught at our recent Heaven Down Business Conference 2.0 and includes revelations from our team. With the exception of personal ministry times to various persons in attendance, and the addition of Chapter 8 on How to Work with Your Angel (taught at our 1.0 Conference), you are reading most of the content of the 2.0 conference. For the most part, the chapters of this book and the revelation it contains were borne out of engagements Donna Neeper (my Executive Assistant) and I had, primarily with Mitchell, a man in white linen who is assigned to our ministry to aid us in our understanding and engagement of Heaven and how it applies specifically to the business arena.

We experienced a powerful presence of Holy Spirit during this conference, with many dynamic things occurring in the lives of the attendees. We trust you will sense the presence of Holy Spirit and the hosts of Heaven as you read this book.

Some of the subject matter you may think you already know, but you have probably never heard it the way you will in this book. Mitchell challenged us, but also liberated us with the instructions he gave us in the many applications of Heaven down living. You will find them liberating as well. As you read, let your spirit absorb what is being shared. Pockets of deep revelation are scattered throughout the chapters. You will see some things in fresh ways, and clarification will come to areas you may have always wondered about. As we share these revelations, may your spirit grasp fully all that Heaven is releasing. As you apply it to your life and business, may you live fully spirit first.

Chapter 1
Wealth Creation

As Donna and I accessed the Business Complex Help Desk, we requested to know what was on the agenda for us that day, which is something we have learned to do. We were introduced to Mitchell, a man in white linen,[5] who was going to instruct us on a few matters. This was to be the first of a series of engagements over the next few weeks that were going to provide life-changing and paradigm-shifting information to us concerning learning how to build a business (or ministry) from Heaven down. I had determined to "practice what I preach" and regularly engage Heaven concerning the building of my ministry, LifeSpring International Ministries, Inc.

We were ushered into a conference room, and he began to speak concerning wealth creation and the

---

[5] Man (or woman) in white linen refers to saints who have already entered Heaven and have been trained by Heaven to assist believers on the earth in various tasks. They always seek to exalt the Father and are never seeking their own glory. Remember that Jesus engaged Moses and Elijah (men in white) on the Mount of Transfiguration.

Father's desire to cause His sons and daughters to become wealth creators in the earth. Many companies exist throughout the earth which are employers of thousands, yet these companies are often founded in league with mammon and have ungodly practices and principles by which they operate. Heaven and our Heavenly Father would like the primary employers of mankind to be His sons and daughters.

We are still in the process of shedding old garments of religiosity, church life, and the way we do church from the old era. To build a business from Heaven down requires new concepts and beliefs, as well as the constant involvement of Heaven and its resources in what we do. We need to realize that we are creators creating with the Creator (God). Even in building a business, as we cooperate with Heaven, we are creating with the Creator. Heaven is working in league with us to accomplish Heaven on earth through the work of our hands. It is us, the creation, creating with the might and power of the Creator himself. This is not a once and done type of thing, but rather a long-term picture of what is coming to the earth through the Bride of Christ.

Mitchell told us that an increased capacity for wealth creation has now been announced to the earth realm by the hosts of Heaven, and we have the privilege to participate with Heaven in this vast venture. I found it to be a prophetic symbol when my book, *Building Your Business from Heaven Down*, reached number one status in the Wealth Management category, outpacing *The University of Berkshire Hathaway: 30 Years of Lessons*

Learned from Warren Buffett & Charlie Munger at the Annual Shareholders Meeting, particularly since Warren Buffett is currently one of the richest men on the planet. We were the number 1 bestseller in the Sales & Selling category on Kindle, too.

In the Old Testament, we can read the record of a widow who was in dire straits. Her income had dried up and she was about to lose her two sons to a creditor, who would enslave them to pay a debt. She was instructed by the prophet Elisha to borrow as many jars and pots as she could from her neighbors. She obeyed Elisha and gathered pots and vessels from friends and neighbors all around her and placed them in her home. Then, following the instruction of Elisha, she brought her two sons in the house and shut the door. She then began to pour olive oil from the flask into each pot until all the pots were full to the brim. Once all the pots were full, the oil stopped flowing. Mitchell implied to us that we could have as much as we were willing to believe for.

How many pots do you have? How much provision can you believe for? In this era, Heaven has given us an invitation. Gather pots so He can fill them.

Put out your pots to receive the revelation of wealth creation.

Will you use wealth for the purposes of the Kingdom of God and its expansion in the earth? That is what Heaven wants to know. We must focus on access to the heavenly realms and Heaven's impartation for us.

Remember, all good things come from above. We must take counsel from the heavenly realms to access this revelation. It cannot be business as usual. It must become *"business Heaven's way!"*

One of the ways you can increase your capacity for revelation is to pray in the spirit using your prayer language. When you pray in the spirit you are building the framework for revelation to abide in.[6] The more you pray in the spirit, the larger and stronger the edifice will be. I encourage you to build a strong framework for revelation in your life.

In early 2020, I was introduced by Heaven to an understanding of the power of spiritual bonds which are legal agreements in the realms of Heaven that can positively impact your life when arising out of Heaven or negatively impact you if arising out of hell. I wrote the book *Releasing Bonds from the Courts of Heaven* out of that revelation. Refer to that book for more information about this powerful understanding. As we were learning from Mitchell the material in this chapter, we were reminded to deal with every ungodly bond against our ministry. I would offer the same advice to you, to deal with every ungodly bond against your ministry. Our ministry has a team of ministry friends who access Heaven on our behalf to deal with the ungodly bonds that have been placed against it (it is a regular occurrence), and to request godly bonds for us. Each

---

[6] Jude 20, 1 Corinthians 14:1-4

team member takes a specific day to do that. We are so grateful for this undergirding of the ministry by these team members. Might I recommend that you gather a few friends and supporters to do the same thing for you and your enterprise? It has been invaluable for us.

Deal with every ungodly bond!

Chapter 2
Pulling Down Strongholds in Business

As we continued our instruction from Mitchell, the subject matter changed to some extremely helpful advice and insight into strongholds that you are likely to encounter with your business.

Part of effectively trading from Heaven is to recognize and dismantle every stronghold against your business. Wealth creation is often resisted by the strongholds of Satan and his rebellious armies, but wealth creation through trade is a gift of the Father to His children. The activity of godly trade keeps Satan disgruntled. Because creativity has been removed from his being, he is even more jealous of the sons and daughters who have stepped into their role and are expressing godly trade in the earth. He unleashes his anger on the activity of trade and the principle of multiplication.

The Tactic of Division

He brings division with the aim of causing disruption to the flow of the activity of multiplication. When you are experiencing growth, understand the Satan's tactic of bringing division to your team so he can stop the multiplication of your business or ministry. It is the same tactic he has been using throughout the centuries to hinder trade.

When Job had a disruption in his ability to trade due to the destruction of his children, the enemy used his "friends" to inflict further damage to Job. Even Job's wife, his covenant companion, was affected, and wanted Job to simply curse God and die. The grief was more than she could bear. This pattern has not changed through the centuries and has not needed to, because humans tend to fall into the same traps. You must see past the deception of the moment. The enemy wants you to place blame or look suspiciously at a co-worker or teammate, all with the aim of disrupting the trade and its multiplication.

Rather than fall for this old trick of Satan's, we should not only circle the wagons (an expression from the old West describing when the settlers would come under attack by their enemies and would form a circle with their covered wagons to create a barricade against the attackers). We need to take an additional step – to forcefully advance during the season of attack. Do *more* of what you do. Determine to do it better, stronger, and more effectively than ever before. Where the enemy has endeavored to slow you down or stop you, as one voice, advance against the enemy.

The Tactic of Empire Building

Another tactic of Satan is to get the leadership of an organization to resort to empire building in order to divert trade and affect the multiplication of the enterprise. Multiplication is a natural result of healthy growth, but in the process of empire building, shortcuts will often be taken that weaken the structure of the organization.

Abraham witnessed this tactic with his nephew Lot. Lot had witnessed Abraham's increase in wealth due to having learned how to operate in the trade routes of Heaven. Lot began to covet Abraham's riches and desired to build his own empire. Abraham was not trying to build an empire; the multiplication he experienced was a natural result of healthy growth. Lot got distracted and got ahead of the process.

It was not long after Abraham and Lot separated that Lot's poor choices began to be seen. He moved to a city (an obvious natural choice to conduct trade – lots of people, right?), but it was a bad move. The people of that city were wicked, and when the men in white came to visit Lot to usher him and his family from the city to safety, Lot offered his daughters to be raped by the men of the city so they would not harm his guests.

Even upon leaving the city, the allure of it was still attractive to Lots wife, who looked back upon the city during its destruction and was suddenly turned to a pillar of salt – a sad and unnecessary ending.

Abraham had demonstrated that you do not need a city to have successful trade. He did not live in a city but in the countryside, and yet he was becoming fabulously wealthy by his obedience.

The Tactic of Bloodline Issues

Pulling down of hindrances and strongholds against businesses is required for a saint's business to prosper. If you do not do it, who will? You must determine the main thrust of opposition against your business. If he cannot divert you in the ways previously described he will use another tactic, the iniquity of the bloodline of the owner, or a key player in the organization, to gain legal ground to disrupt the business.

If you have not diligently pursued getting the iniquity issues of your bloodline cleansed personally, do not wait another day. Remember, the enemy will use your bloodline issues or that of key individuals in your organization to disrupt your business. It would be of value to you, as the owner, to assist your management team in getting their generational issues cleared. We have a lot of material on our website and in our books related to that subject that can aid you in clearing these things so your business can have maximum success.

Do not ignore the potential impact of Freemasonry in your bloodline or the bloodline of those in your leadership team. Satan will outflank you with things of this nature and cause major damage to your business. It may be that you and your team have already dealt with the generational issues but realize that it is an ongoing process to get clean and stay clean. The enemy would love to interfere by causing inter-office romances of an ungodly nature to crop up. Keep your spiritual shields up against the various tactics of the enemy.

Creating a No-Go Zone

Give NO PLACE to gossip and slander, whether of others on your team, employees, contractors, vendors, or customers. Keep those arenas "no go zones" for your business. As an organization, simply do NOT engage in gossip, slander, or accusation. Rather, be busy blessing and speaking blessing over your team, your customers, and your suppliers.

Spiritual Ignorance

Satan also may play on the spiritual ignorance of those in the organization, including employees, and use that as a method of deception, to bring them into agreement with lies. If Satan cannot mess with you, he will keep looking until he finds someone whom he can. Invest in the spiritual growth of your employees. Pay attention to the signs of trouble. They may be dealing with things at home that are affecting their work performance. Be aware of patterns that are unhealthy in their lives or performance.

Ungodly Bonds to Cloud Vision

Satan may simply register ungodly bonds that bring clouding, confusion, double-mindedness, and division to the leadership of an organization. As mentioned earlier, you need to deal with the ungodly bonds but also request the release of godly bonds in the lives of your employees and on behalf of your business entity.

Clouding focus, vision, goal-oriented dreams, and memory loss of why one is multiplying and trading in the first place are some of his favorites. If the enemy can cloud your focus, obscure your vision or dreams, or cause you to forget why you are doing what you do, he will be able to bring serious harm to your business. A veil over the eyes of leadership is a serious plot and stronghold against business.

If there is unrighteousness that he can divert the trade into, he will attempt to do so. Satan will be persistent in seeking ways to interrupt your business. Keep tabs on the spiritual atmosphere and climate of your business. Be aware of the little nudges of Holy Spirit or your angel indicating that something is amiss, or that the enemy is afoot in some fashion against your business. This often comes through greed, overstepping one's bounds, moving boundaries of other partners, and operating in league with darkness.

As a business, my Executive Assistant and I will access the Business Complex almost daily. We will request to see what is on Heaven's calendar for us that day and then follow Heaven's instructions.

Sometimes we are directed to the Personnel Department where Heaven will apprise us of concerns related to our team. We may need to release bonds for some of them or release blessings to them. Sometimes we are made aware of activities within the team that can be potentially disruptive. Having a heads up from Heaven is invaluable.

At times Heaven has instructed us to request things for our employees' personal angels, which we have done with wonderful results. We are quite aware of cooperating with the ministry angel and encourage our team to do the same, but it may be overlooked by them, so we are able to help the employee out by requesting some things for their angel so that angel can do their job more effectively.

Pride and Competition

Satan may resort to the use of pride, which leads to competition that disrupts the business. Pride and competition make it easy for the devil, and he does not have to work as hard. Pride will make you competitive, but it will also blind you to the true issues that need to be dealt with. Your employees can engage in a godly level of friendly competitiveness, but you need to keep watch so that it does not cross the line into an ungodly competition. A familiar verse for each of us to remember is:

> *Pride goes before destruction, And a haughty spirit before a fall. Proverbs 16:18*

Let us keep pride at bay in our personal lives and in the culture of our businesses. God can do a lot more with humility than He can with pride.

The Seed Thief

Satan does not care what you are trading on as much as he cares about where it is easy for him to gain legal right to cloud vision, cause disruption, or prevent the expansion of seed. If he can steal your seed and has a legal right to do so, you will eventually come to ruination. A foundation stone of a business must be the dedication of it to the Lord with intent of desire and will to operate within the boundary lines the Father has established.

The trade of Heaven that a business owner has is with Heaven. If you do not yet have a business but have an idea that you hope will one day become a business which causes trade and multiplication, whether a physical object, a service, or intellectual property from the thought realm, the original trade of this individual is with Heaven.

The Declaration of Trade

Obtaining a Declaration of Trade is imperative! In my book, *Building Your Business from Heaven Down* I write about the importance of this document and in the next chapter I will cover more details as well. Realize you must have this document in place to fully engage your business and be locked in with Heaven.

Are You Hardwired?

Some individuals are hardwired for business in their DNA, and along their path of growth, that saint would receive a cleansing of DNA simply because they are engaged in what they need to be. When you are walking out your purpose, you have access to a continual flow of cleansing that will work in your life on every level. Your spiritual maturity level will grow as you grow in the activity of your hands.

Sometimes this happens from a young age. The desire to multiply, expand, and grow is in many of God's children, even before their spirit is awakened to Him. The wiring in their DNA, combined with the words written in the scroll of their life, can often lead them into these areas from young ages, such as the children's lemonade stands on the corners of their neighborhoods.

The Father desires to bless many businesses across the spectrum of trade but it must begin in Heaven.

All things begin in Heaven

Beginning in Heaven first is how businesses should operate, but it has been greatly resisted and even co-opted by darkness. Knowledge of the strongholds mentioned earlier is a starting place for recognizing of what pitfalls to watch for along the way as a business is being established.

Heaven desires to help you overcome in every aspect of your business so that you are not wearied by trade, but find enjoyment, pleasure, and lightness of the Father in it.

Foundation stones are extremely important. What you build upon makes a difference in the outcome of what is built. Be aware. You do not have to be in fear, but you do need to be aware of these pitfalls to guard against them and utilize the resources of Heaven to see them overcome. The next few chapters will explain some of these foundation stones.

Enjoy doing business from Heaven!

Chapter 3
The Declaration of Trade
& Deed of Commerce & Trade

In my bestselling book, *Building Your Business from Heaven Down*, I wrote about a document called the Declaration of Trade. More understanding concerning this document came as we engaged with Mitchell. He further explained several things that will help clarify what I did not cover in that book.

The Declaration of Trade must be requested in the Court of Titles and Deeds[7] in order for a ruling to be given to the saint stating they have the right of Heaven and Heaven's agreement to trade in their activity. Simply requesting a Declaration of Trade is not usually enough. A Declaration of Trade establishes who you are, what the business is, what it does, and who it trades on behalf of.

---

[7] In the book, *Building Your Business from Heaven Down* I mention that the Declaration of Trade can be obtained in the Court of Records. Mitchell clarified that the Court of Titles and Deeds is the preferred venue for obtaining this document as it also included the Deed of Commerce and Trade.

The Declaration of Trade provides Heaven's authorization to do business. It is Heaven's Seal of Approval.

Establish Your Boundaries

The Declaration of Trade establishes the boundaries of your business (what you do and who your audience is). You define your market or audience so you can stake your claim.

The Declaration of Trade establishes your right to conduct business according to Kingdom guidelines. It declares your right to conduct business both in the realms of Heaven and on the earth. It assigns angels to your enterprise and it is the foundational document for your business. It establishes what you must trade, how you will trade, where you will trade, and what method(s) you will use to trade.

Establish Headship

The Declaration of Trade establishes the Father's headship, and it establishes your headship over your enterprise. The one who is the most senior in the partnership and the most spiritually mature can request the Declaration of Trade on behalf of the entity.

Dedication to the LORD is first.

Your business truly becomes a Kingdom enterprise by your dedication of the business to the LORD of Hosts. You are entering into a partnership with Heaven to conduct your business. He is first, you are second.

Establish the Pattern

With the Declaration of Trade, you agree to trade according to the principles of the Father. You agree to trade with:

- Righteousness
- Justice
- Fairness
- Just Weights and Balances
- Honoring of Property Rights
- The Principle of Knowing and Staying in Your Boundaries
- The Principle of Knowing Your Sphere.

You must endeavor to build it as one who has inherited the Kingdom. You also agree to receive the counsel given to you by Heaven. It establishes your partnership with Heaven. It will establish the LORD of Hosts as the ultimate owner of your enterprise and will establish your position of headship in it as well.

Receive the Resources

Heaven's resources await release for you. Resources of every kind, not just earthly and not just heavenly. Once your Declaration of Trade is approved, your angel(s) are released to your business and your accounts are established in the Finance, Creative and Personnel Departments in the Business Complex of Heaven.

Once you access the Court of Titles and Deeds and request the Declaration of Trade, often the answer and the ruling to the request is positive, except in cases where individuals are not ready due to spiritual immaturity, or other details regarding the business need clarification. Also, the Father is aware of how easily pride and greed may enter the picture, so the request of the establishment to trade may be denied on those bases.

If approved, the Declaration of Trade is signed off by Heaven and it becomes the initial trade of that business. When you receive your Declaration of Trade, be sure to record the date.

Often, when requesting the Declaration of Trade, the business owner has not fully thought through the legal structure they will need to operate from in the natural. Heaven will have suggestions or considerations for them so they can maximize what they do in the earth while minimizing their personal risk or financial exposure. Take Heaven's advice, get counsel first and then, when you have decided, you can access the Court of Titles and Deeds and proceed to obtain the Declaration of Trade along with the Deed of Commerce & Trade.

Retroactive Establishment

What if you missed obtaining your Declaration of Trade first? Sometimes people have already established their business but never obtained their Declaration of Trade from Heaven. That is quite often the case, as it was not known about until recently. Grace and mercy are available so that it can be done outside of a linear timeline. You can simply access the Court of Titles and Deeds and request your Declaration of Trade be granted retroactively to the time of its origin (i.e. the date of incorporation). If you need to go back in time to adjust that, this would be a place to begin.

Because you are initializing this with Heaven, every firstborn is the Lord's and it is dedicated to the Lord. The first fruit of this is the first fruit of your trade, and it represents your trade with Heaven.

The Declaration of Trade is a legal document that is obtained in the Courts of Heaven, but it is also a trade *with* Heaven. The first fruit of receiving the Declaration of Trade is the grace and mercy necessary concerning your enterprise. Each enterprise, whether business or ministry, has a measure of grace and mercy needed to function. The establishment of the business by the Declaration of Trade opens the door to release of that grace and mercy to your entity. The first fruit of your businesses' multiplication is to receive from Heaven the first trade, which is the Declaration of Trade packaged with that grace and mercy.

Many things in the background of Heaven then begin to come to fruition for the business itself. Angels are assigned, scrolls are written, space is made in Heaven for your trading floor, you are given access to the Business Complex of Heaven, your account in the Finance Department is set up with all the appropriate measures, including your representative in that department and your ATM card for access to the resources of Heaven for your business.

Heaven begins an accounting of your business from the date of its establishment, via the Declaration of Trade, to tally up and measure out trades, resources of Heaven, and all the accounting of Heaven and how all of that plays into various aspects of what you would call business.

Your space in the Creative Department is also allocated, along with the needed resources for you and your leadership of your organization. This appears in the Business Complex and you are put on the schedule at the Help Desk, which has been hoping you would enter the realms of Heaven.

Night dreaming begins for the individual. Be sure to access Donna's materials on capturing your dreams.[8] You may also want to avail yourself of the Dream Capture Journal we have available on our website (www.courtsofheaven.net). You will find that, within these dreams, Heaven will be speaking to you concerning your business. New ideas, inventions, methods, new clients, releases of favor, and more can all come out of these encounters with Heaven in the night. This is the mercy of the Father for those desiring to gather corporately to advance seed to harvest, with the outcome being multiplication.

---

[8] Donna taught on this in the Building Your Business from Heaven Down 1.0 Web Conference. Video access is available at our website: www.courtsofheavenwebinars.com.

Deed of Commerce and Trade

An additional document you receive is called the Deed of Commerce and Trade. A deed entitles you to a place. In this case, the Deed of Commerce and Trade creates a trading floor on behalf of your business in Heaven, from which you are to conduct the trades of your business. It grants you a deed to the place of trade. Think of the trading floor as both a place and an activity.

What you accomplished by obtaining the Declaration of Trade and the Deed of Commerce and Trade was attaining Heaven's agreement with your desire to trade from Heaven down.

"Are the Declaration of Trade & the Deed of Commerce and Trade the same thing?" we asked?

We were told that they are two pages of the same document. You need both. Together, they grant you access to both the trade activities of Heaven and to the place of trade in Heaven, which is a dimensional place tied to your specific entity. It is the cornerstone trade of your business or ministry, and it holds a place of honor. Everything built in your business from this point forward is now linked to this cornerstone trade. Without it, you would not have a starting place upon which to build. It is considered a foundational document. You cannot fully move ahead without it.

Heaven wants your business to start off on the right foot or to be reestablished according to Heaven down principles. We will learn more about how the Heaven down paradigm is key in the coming chapters.

Chapter 4
The Primacy of Heaven

When you have your authorization from Heaven to do business through the receipt of your Declaration of Trade, nuances will accompany every trade because you have traded from Heaven first. These nuances give you an edge over those who operate outside of Heaven first and Heaven down.

Satan recognizes an organization or business that is trading from Heaven first or with Heaven first, and he will look for easier prey. When you trade from Heaven first, your trades in the natural are eased.

[17] And He is before all things, and in Him all things consist. [18] And He is the head of the body, the church, who is the beginning, the firstborn from the dead, that in all things He may have the preeminence. Colossians 1:17-18

The government of God begins in Heaven and applies to every arena of life, businesses included. I am speaking primarily to business owners, but if you are the leader of a ministry, that is also a business. It simply trades in different ways than a shoe store might.

The initiation of the Heaven down paradigm in a business enables the saint to make the trades based upon all the things that are written in Heaven for that entity. Heaven has your business and its growth mapped out. You simply need to discover it.

> *For we are His workmanship, created in Christ Jesus for good works, which God prepared beforehand that we should walk in them. Ephesians 2:10*

When the Heaven down paradigm is operational in your business, everything begins to come into alignment. This alignment will not just be in business, but also in your family life, as well as your personal life. Mitchell informed us that the unredeemed parts of a saint are more easily or readily worked out through the process of growth and change when the application of trade from Heaven down has first priority. This is in keeping with the promise of God found in Matthew.

> *So above all, constantly chase after the realm of God's kingdom and the righteousness that proceeds from him. Then all these less important things will be given to you abundantly. Matthew 6:33 (TPT)*

You probably know it as:

Seek first the kingdom of God and His righteousness (way of doing things), and all these things shall be added to you. Matthew 6:33

Put the Kingdom first!

Seeking first the kingdom of God releases angels on behalf of your business. Once you have started on this journey, come back regularly and request to know what the next step is of building the business.

Heaven has more knowledge than you and your realm!

The flow of revelation in business is a coming attraction and those in the earth realm are going to come to know it because this is the time for it.

This is our freedom!

Begin of the Flow of Favor

This waterfall of favor from Heaven comes down on the area of natural transaction, trade, and commerce, and it begins to raise the water level of the Spirit within the natural arena.

How do you prime that waterfall? You do so by constantly accessing the realms of Heaven concerning your business and your relationship with the Father. When your spirit has first place over your soul and is instructing your soul, you will tithe, you will give first fruits, you will give offerings, and you will follow all the instructions of Heaven related to your business. You will want to follow them because of the favor of God released in such abundance to you. You will think like God. You will have the mind of Christ.

Your obedience in every area primes the flow of Heaven down wealth because all wealth comes from Heaven down.

All wealth comes from Heaven down

Your obedience to instruction enables you to carry the wealth coming from Heaven, but you will not retain it for yourself. You will disperse the blessings, causing a multiplication in your business which will affect everything around you.

A rising tide lifts all boats

Release the vertical relationship of Heaven, which is done through hope, expectation, and faith via tithes, offerings, first fruits, alms...anything to do with money. (We will talk more about that in the next chapter.)

Let your spirit speak! Your spirit is already primed to know how obey God. Give way to your spirit.

*That which you hold on to
is what you trust in.*

Satan's original sin was that he held the glory to himself instead of releasing it to the Lord. His role was to be a releaser of glory to God. He began to covet that glory and sought to withhold it from the Father. It did not work out well for him.

Yahweh is a Multiplier.

He created mankind to multiply like himself and He is limitless in his multiplication capacity. Saints in commerce, trade, and business are will need to make sure they are locked in to the limitlessness of God

---
God wants to bless your business

Allow God to be fully involved in your business. Run your business according to biblical principles, the heart of God, the mind of Christ, and the co-laboring spirit of a human with the spirit of God.

Lessons from Monopoly

Recently, Donna was with some of her family enjoying time together. One of their favorite things to do is play board games. This particular night, Donna suggested speed Monopoly, so they set out the game and began to play. The game had progressed for a short while when Donna suddenly became aware of her angel standing near her. The angel whispered to her to speak aloud what she wanted from the roll of the dice when it was her turn to play. As it became her time to roll the dice she spoke "I don't want to land on the yellow, green, or purple spaces." She rolled the dice and missed each of those spaces. Incidentally, some of these spaces had houses and hotels on them, which can be expensive properties to land and pay rent on. Donna continued this pattern for 18 times at play during that game, much to the amazement of the others playing with her.

Donna knew that this was highly unusual, so later she asked her angel what the lesson was. The angels reply was, "To teach you about the Father's favor!" The favor of the Father was demonstrated through a simple board game that night to Donna, along with a few other lessons she learned:

- Do not hold your cards too tightly
- Do not think you own something-it is all rented
- Go with Heaven's solution –even if it does not seem to make sense at first
- Patience, diligence, faith, and perseverance will be required
- Realize that it is a boat, NOT a building
- Expect favor
- Be bold and let your spirit speak!

Donna also learned in another way that when you collaborate with the angels, they operate from the higher dimension of the supernatural.

The longer we have been immersed in church culture, the more religious we tend to get. We sometimes feel that we must pepper our conversations with "Christianeze" and always throw in pet phrases like "Glory to God, Hallelujah, and Thank you Jesus!" and the like. Instead of being an attractor to God they become a detractor.

Do not get religiousy!

God will get the ultimate glory! He does not necessarily need our help either.

You cannot do business from church – the religious church – as you have known it.

The lifestyle of living from Heaven down is available to anyone who will choose it. Heaven would love to work with you to get God glory because as we live in this manner it gives Him glory. Remember to keep it simple. It does not have to be complicated. Do not wait another day! Start today!

Chapter 5
First Fruits & Tithes

Creating trade relationships is first accomplished through our pocketbooks. After discussing the spiritual things that need to be done, Mitchell took the conversation in a vastly different direction than I had anticipated. He began to speak concerning first fruits, and the conversation morphed into the whole arena of first fruits, tithes, offerings, and alms and how they are tightly knit with building a business. Tithing, alms giving, and first fruit giving all are accounted in Heaven on your behalf or on behalf of the entity through which you give.

Tithes

He explained the tithe in this manner. The tithe is a portion given by a person in obedience to the command of the Father as recorded in scripture. It is proof of the persons dependence upon the Father. Heaven keeps an accounting of ones' tithing so that recognition can be made in Heaven. Malachi 3 records that one of the benefits of the tithe is that the devourer (seed eater) would be rebuked for your sake. One of the purposes of the tithe (which means tenth) is to provide for the priests.

The tithe is recognized in Heaven on behalf of the one tithing and is essential for the establishment of the covenant on behalf of the tither. It has the promise of blessing to the tither as recorded in Malachi 3, where we are told the windows of Heaven would be open to us via the tithe. It is essential for an open Heaven.

Tithing creates recognition on the part of the saint of Heaven's right to their affairs. Tithing also creates protection for you from mammon or the love of money. Tithing and taxing are correlated, as the tithe is a tax on trade.

First Fruits

We asked Mitchell to explain first fruits in more detail, which he was pleased to do. He explained that first fruits are a preferred form of giving because it comes from love and an expectation of the goodness of God. It comes from a sincerity of trust in the name of Jehovah Jireh as provider. It is a trade and a storing up for future blessing released by Heaven at the right time. First fruits are an opportunity of faith to store up seed in heavenly storehouses in advance of the culmination of trade.

First fruits are a heartfelt connection to worship that creates a trade in the heavenlies. It is the expectation of the goodness of God to give more than you put in. First fruits are a trade by faith where your seed multiplies in

Heaven's storehouses and an expression of love. The contrast between tithing and the giving of first fruits is a matter of the heart. Heaven wants first fruits to be given of your own volition, whereas tithing is a response of obedience. First fruits is essentially trading with Heaven first.

The trading floor created by first fruit offerings is multi-dimensional and has multiple expressions. This is not easy to explain but rather needs to be experienced. What makes Heaven happy is the giving of the first fruit in a marked time.

You have the opportunity to avail yourself of the first fruit offering. Paying the tithe is a step of obedience. The tithe is called the grace of God because the grace of God enabled the initial tribes of Israel to survive in the desert.

What makes first fruit different from tithe is the motivation of the heart. Tithes and first fruits are both trade relationships because they are counted in Heaven. However, tithing can be done without the heart involved.

Making trades with Heaven must be primary.

When trading from Heaven first, what manifests in the natural is linked to the activity of Heaven. It is releasing an expectation of the goodness of the Father in total trust and is a type of sacrifice. It is the seed of increase. First fruits should come with a recognition of honor and respect for the one from whom all good things flow, the Father of lights.

In business, a first fruit offering is a release from the heart, with the givers' expectation, that stakes a claim for the Father's provision in the activity to which it is linked.

It must be representative of the increase you expect.

Holy Spirit work can work with you to help you understand this. Your agreement with this is from the heart and based on your relationship with God who is good, and the God who gives everything. First fruits giving pulls on the grace of God. It is sacrificial because you are giving *before* the increase shows up. First fruits is a type of sacrifice with the expectation that your portion will be there.

Speak over your seed!

What you speak over it as you give determines what it is linked to, and this accrues in Heaven.

Declaration Over Your First Fruits Seed

Lord, out of my present amount, I give to you the release of my trust and release of my faith, and the release in thanksgiving that you are good and you are wise and I will see this come back to me in the form of _____ state your desired result _____.

This trade is accounted for in Heaven. That is the beauty of an offering of first fruits. The reason it engages the heart is because it touches the soul. The soul is aware that it gives from its current and present situation and must engage faith *in* the spirit *with* the spirit.

Alms

Alms is the Father's heart for the poor. It is the release of kindness toward others. You may sense yourself walking in a blessing and you release out of that blessing to another human.

Your alms giving can be to release funds, recommendations, or kind words toward another business. For instance, suppose you own a print shop and there is one down the block which is not doing as well as you. You, out of thanksgiving to the Father, could begin to recommend them to clients who come to you, since you are so busy. You put in a kind word for that print shop. It may not be directly monetary, but it will be a form of blessing toward them.

Alms comes from recognizing a blessing that wants to release to another so that the blessing is multiplied in a similar situation. Alms do not have to be financial. At LifeSpring, we regularly provide complimentary personal and business advocacy sessions to those in need. This is a form of alms giving for our ministry and causes multiplication of it. We do not directly give it FOR the multiplication, but we understand that it is a result of that form of giving. Essentially, this is what Galatians 6:7 is saying:

> *A man's harvest in life will depend entirely upon what he sows. Galatians 6:7 (Phillips)*

Offerings

Offerings is a type of giving separate from the tithe, first fruits, or alms. An offering is a release out of your increase to where the demonstration of the Kingdom has been. It is a marker of the Lord.

All things are marked by what spoken over it in the act of giving.

What you are speaking over it is recorded and accrued in Heaven. The release of the harvest becomes easier for you. Remember that all gifts should be given cheerfully. If not, it does not honor the Father. However, responding – to the unction of the Spirit, the movement of the angelic around you, the weighty glory that causes people to give that will settle in a place on a group of people – is crucial. Offerings and first fruits are very much tied to the heart and what you speak over them because it is a gift for you to be able to speak over them and will be the harvest that the seed is connected to.

You always want your offerings to be given to a ministry, a church, or some other entity that has demonstrations of the Kingdom being expressed. They have revelatory flow coming from the ministry, lives are being impacted, needs are being met, etc. Just as a responsible farmer would not make it a practice to sow his seed in poor, nutrient-deficient soil, so you, as the one making the offering, should sow responsibly. Is that church or ministry fulfilling their part of the Great Commission? Do you see good fruit coming out of that ministry?

We also must understand that once we sow the seed, the harvest it produces it up to the Father, not us. We have released the gift in faith and spoken over it with full expectation of abundant harvest. After that, it is simply a matter of time before the harvest is reaped from the seed sown.

Wounded Givers

Unfortunately, many in the Body of Christ have been wounded in their giving. The principles of first fruits, tithes, offerings, or alms may have been greatly abused. Our challenge is to maintain an open heart to the Father and let Holy Spirit heal our wounds related to giving.

When you give, you are taking something from the natural realm and transacting something that is unseen, spiritual, and supernatural. We must allow the truth of giving to be instilled within us and allow Holy Spirit to minister to both soul and spirit so that new alignments and pathways of thoughts can begin to build a new temple within our minds on these topics.

> *The abuse of an issue does not discount the truth of an issue.*

Although painful at times, these types of conversations are necessary for walls that have been built as a result of wounds to be torn down within the life of a believer. It is regrettable how the enemy has stolen the glory of God by making the people of God feel they owe God.

> *When your spirit has first place over your soul and is instructing your soul, you will tithe, you will give first fruits, you will give offerings, and alms.*

The enemy's intent through the misguided teachings you may have previously heard was to position you to no longer trust your Heavenly Father. For some people, he succeeded, and they have closed that area of their lives off to healing and correction. Sometimes the motives of the ones teaching us were problematic, and (let us be honest) sometimes our own motives for giving were questionable. God is not a vending machine, and the principles of the Kingdom concerning giving and receiving must be honored in our lives as well.

We may have been coerced into giving or had our arms twisted by someone's appeal. God will deal with them. Our responsibility is to forgive them, bless them, and release them from the negative impact they had upon our lives.

If you need healing pertaining to giving, simply acknowledge that you need healing in that area and ask Holy Spirit to begin the healing process for you. You need not let past hurts stop you from future blessings.

Remember, that which you hold on to is what you trust in.

What is our trust in?

Chapter 6
Creative Downloads

One of the first things that opens up to a business owner is the Creative Department of the Business Complex of Heaven. Because I discuss the details of the Creative Department in my previous book, *Building Your Business from Heaven Down*, I will simply address some highlights here.

When we access the Creative Department, we are tapping into the creative flow of Heaven. Permission is granted to allow your creative spirit to take the forefront. Begin to ask yourself, "What could I invent?"

Sometimes what blocks creativity is the thought that any idea must be a big idea, so we dismiss smaller ideas as insignificant. I want to give you permission to flow with the small idea. *Stop pre-judging your ideas.* You have permission to suspend judgment.

Allow yourself – give yourself permission – to receive the small idea

You are designed to visualize, create, and process ideas. You have gotten this far in this book so you may as well jump all the way in the river of understanding of these things. I give you permission to jump in the river completely. Allow yourself time to think creatively. Allow your spirit to explore possibilities and ideas. Let your spirit rethink what you do!

Creativity IS business!

Pre-judging comes from conformity of and to the world. You have permission to "color outside the lines." Paul admonished us in Romans 12:2:

*Don't let the world around you **squeeze you into its own mold**, but let God re-mold your minds from within, so that you may prove in practice that the plan of God for you is good, meets all his demands and moves towards the goal of true maturity. (Phillips) (Emphasis mine)*

Instead, remake the mold. Ask the simple question, "What if?" Rethink your industry or business. Rethink your ways of doing business. Is what you are doing now doing well? It can do better – rethink it!

Part of the Heaven down strategy is getting the flow in the right direction – *from* Heaven downward. It is meant to be a vertical flow, not a horizontal flow. Not from the bottom to the top, but from the top to the bottom.

---
*Set aside fear that you
will be judged for your idea*

Heaven is not judging you about your idea. Heaven wants to release more and more creativity to you and inside of you. Realize that you are predestined for this!

Get in and stay in your flow! As you do, hope and expectation will come. The 3-D realm is always conforming. Think about it. Why do ALL fast food restaurants look the same? If you look at a McDonald's, Burger King, Wendy's, Chick-Fil-A, or Arby's – notice the color scheme. They are all earth toned colors with an accent of either red or yellow or both.

McDonald's originally came into prominence because they built a better way of serving the customers, Chick-Fil-A has come to prominence because of their excellent customer service. It is too bad some of the other fast-food franchises have not taken more lessons from Chick-Fil-A.

---
*Your conformed thoughts
cause your pre-judgments*

Find Your Time

Realize that the flow of creativity is stronger in the morning than in the afternoon. Generally, you are most refreshed in the morning, so it would help you to develop a pattern of allowing time for creative flow then before the day gets going too much. Make it a habit as something you cannot afford to do without because you really cannot. Remember the retailer, K-Mart? They became large because they did the large variety store concept better than competitors of the time. Then, Wal-Mart came along and did a similar thing even better. Whereas K-Mart once was prominent, Walmart now holds that position in the marketplace. Amazon is now redefining the marketplace and unless Walmart steps up its game in the online ordering arena, they too will be a part of the landscape of retail history. They have every reason to maintain their market dominance because they have far more outlets that could be adapted to servicing customers online than Amazon has. However, Amazon is outpacing them in distribution. Similar stories have been played out over and over again in business in nearly every country around the globe. So, ask yourself, "What if...?" How could we do what we do better? What emerging opportunities await?

Chapter 7
Mind Mapping with a Twist

Heaven has NO limit of creativity for you. Limitations do not exist – not in Heaven, anyway. One of the reasons for the Creative Department's existence is to help you clear away the misconceptions about creativity and the power of dreaming.

The Dreaming Room

In the Creative Department, each business has a drawer. These drawers contain sensory objects to help you dream. They may appear as Legos, Play-Doh, toys, balls, and other things of that nature. They serve a purpose. The intention is for you to take an object like the ones mentioned above, get in a relaxed position, close your eyes, and begin to manipulate it by faith for the tactile sensation. This can help unlock creativity lying dormant within you. You can do this in the Dreaming Rooms within the Creative Department where you come to dream by faith. In these rooms, you can choose the sound frequency needed to assist your creativity. In the natural, you would not play Metallica to get in a relaxed frame of mind. Heaven understands that dynamic. If you are unsure what to listen to, ask the attendant in that department for recommendations.

Begin to mull over what you came to think about while using the toys for tactile stimulation and receive whatever flows into your mind. Jot down the new ideas. Be childlike. Let your spirit soar! Do not consider anything to be too outrageous.

Thinking Room

Within the Creative Department, you will also find the Thinking Room. Upon entering, tell the attendant the general topic that you are interested in writing about. They may bring you a book, a box, a folder, a computer, or tablet; whatever they deem necessary to assist you in your time in the Thinking Room.

No matter what subject you are interested in, you can begin to look and see or hear and listen for the framework or the details of the idea. Details about the potential focus or audience may come forth. The specific topic may arise or questions that this idea answers may come forth during your time in the Thinking Room.

Inventive Room

Not unlike the Thinking Room, you would enter the Creative Department and request to enter the Inventive Room. Tell the attendant the general topic you are considering and begin to engage with what they bring you on the topic. They may bring you blueprints, parts, pieces of something, or any number of things to help you in the process.

> *All ideas that come from the realms of Heaven are always expanding.*

These ideas are always increasing and being added to in Heaven because the things that come from Heaven have a revelation that continuously expands.

Mind Mapping (With a Twist)

Many are familiar with the concept of mind-mapping. In the case of the Heaven down paradigm, we are disengaging our mind and allowing our spirit to take the lead. All the knowledge you need concerning your business is already available. A mind map will help release it to you so you can build on that information. I have put it into simple steps to help your process.

Step 1

Gather:

- Blank sheet of paper (or poster board) & pen(s)
- Timer (use your phone)
- Write your business concept in the center
- Circle it
- Draw lines radiating from the circle
- Set the timer for 15 minutes

Step 2

- Go "spirit forward"[9]
- Step into Heaven
    - At the end of the jutting lines write all the related ideas for your business concept (these become your subtopics)
- Draw lines from the subtopics
- Record the ideas that come from the subtopics

Remember, it does not have to be:

- Pretty
- Organized
- "Right"

It will be:

- Messy – arrows, circles, lists, single phrases or words, misspellings, unfinished thoughts
- Write the obvious
- Write the potentially ridiculous or unfathomable
- Go until you cannot think of anything else. If your 15 minutes runs out, reset the alarm for another 15 minutes.

A mind map is a way to visually organize many ideas. It allows you to place idea after idea in a cohesive form that can eventually be structured. Structuring comes

---

[9] Going "spirit forward" is when we speak to our soul to back up and allow our spirit to come forward and be the dominant aspect of our being.

later. This is for idea formation, not structuring. Have fun!

Chapter 8
How to Work with Your Angel
Part 1

It works like radar. Just as a submarine would detect an object on a radar screen, it works similarly with angels. Thus Ezekiel, our ministry's angel, began his instruction to us.

"Does the angel have me on radar, or do I have an angel on radar," Donna inquired?

Ezekiel replied that it works both ways. Your angel always knows where you are, as if the angel can see you on radar. Wherever that angel is, whatever the angel is doing, the angel is aware of where you are and what you are doing via the angel's radar. It is not quite like a submarine radar screen, but that gives you an idea of how it works. Ezekiel was helping us recognize that this is the method angels use. They have that ability.

"So, you are saying we can learn to use this same sonar pathway or frequency of wave link communication to tune into where you are?" we asked.

"That is what you have to use," was his reply. Whenever you need angelic help, need the presence of Heaven, or need the near presence of the Father, the Son or the Holy Spirit, an angel can bring that to you.

Angels bring various things. To you, it feels like The Presence of the Holy Spirit, but that is really a result of your inability to discern the different levels of The Presence. It is the same thing as a child of God and a maturing saint, beginning to discern different anointings or different expressions of The Presence, and the angels are involved in this.

You can grow in your understanding and your discerning of spirits and what the angels bring. You can discern angels that bring a healing anointing, angels that bring a fire anointing, angels that bring revelation, and anointing angels, and while you may not perceive the angel, you are perceiving the anointing. You are perceiving what they bring or what they carry. What you are really perceiving is their frequency waves.

A healing angel has a different frequency than a revelation angel or a fire angel and you are perceiving them by frequency. Often people are trying to look for them when **they need to discern them first via frequency**. It is easier to do it that way. The auditory and visual frequencies are different.

"I discern them, and after my discernment, then I can look. And usually, as I look in the spirit realm, I begin to get the details of what the angel was like," Donna described to me.

You have a radar function in your spirit that discerns the presence of angels, and most believers do but have never activated it. They do not know how to use it. It would be like handing the car keys to an infant and all the infant knows to do with them is to put them in its mouth. It is a marker of the growth of one's spirit through the spiritual understanding of the spirit realm in Jesus Christ, and the boldness to enter that realm, leaving fear behind.

"You are going to get it wrong on occasion, but that is part of the learning and growing process," Ezekiel said with a smile.

What You Seek, You Find

When you seek for the Father with all your heart, you are going to find the Father. You are going to find his realm. You are going to get what you seek for. If you are seeking for darkness, you are going to get darkness. If you are seeking for light, you are going to get light.

"Do you see the employment of your faith here?" Ezekiel asked. "You face forward from your spirit. You are looking for the Kingdom of Light. The access point is always Jesus. Therefore, the access point is usually praise and as you praise, your spirit comes forward, your soul recedes, and you can employ your spiritual discernment better," he continued.

Some do have the ability to see, seemingly with their natural sight – their natural eyeball. They use their natural eyeball to see angels or to see in the spirit realm, but they are seeing with both sights, spiritual and natural. Your spiritual sight is connected on some level to your natural sight. However, when a person is dying, they may sense them more readily because other senses are already shutting down and as other senses are shutting down prior to death, one's spiritual sight often increases.

You discern through your sensor – your knower. You have discerned numerous angels – single individual angels as well as groups of angels at times. They may not have looked like the pictures in Guidepost or Angels magazines, but you have seen them.

When an angel wants to be made known, it *will* be made known. Some angels are present with you at times, but they are intentionally hiding themselves from your discerner or your knower for a variety of reasons. Some angels need you to acknowledge their presence, however. They are present and they need your understanding and your engagement with them.

"Is that like co-laboring?" Donna asked?

Ezekiel replied in the affirmative and went on to explain that it is a form of co-laboring. As Ezekiel was speaking, he reminded Donna of an example of this that occurred a few days before when she was on a Zoom call with several friends. As she was praying and releasing bonds into a situation and severing bonds a huge angel presented himself to Donna. That angel needed her to discern its presence so that this prayer group could release the angel to do its work, which is exactly what they did.

In fact, when that angel stepped in, Donna asked the angel, "What do I need to do?" He instructed her to release him to do his work, and she knew when the angel left.

The Power of Desire

"Can everybody operate in that?" we wanted to know?

Everyone can to some degree, based on their desire. Sometimes this is called their hunger to do so, based on their curiosity and awakening to the realms of the spirit. Sooner or later, they are going to hunger and thirst after the activity of operating with angels because this is the Father's design, that that the realm of the spirit and angels would work with the realm of the earth and children of God. There are many more angels at work in the earth realm than are being perceived or discerned.

"Is there some way we can help jumpstart that with people?" we asked.

Ezekiel replied, "Teach people that their angels hearken to them more than they are aware." Angels are often assigned to assist the growing awakening of the saint. Your angel has likely been at work helping you become awakened to his or her presence. If you asked to be awakened to their presence, it was your angel who facilitated you asking to be awakened. That was the work of the angel.

Finding the Fear

To help people cooperate with their angel(s), begin by having them comb through their understanding of angels and begin to form questions about what they are afraid of. Fear in any dimension, whether in thought, heart belief, experiences as a youth, or dimensional presences that you did not know the source of, can result in fear being embraced, even if not intentionally.

Where do you have a personal fear of seeing angels? It may be very subtle. You may have been tricked by the enemy to think that you might see a demon instead! If you have asked the Father to see your angel, He will be glad to respond and facilitate that for you.

Once you have identified any fear associated with seeing angels or seeing in the realm of the Spirit, submit the fear to the Father for cleansing and purification. Then request a fresh flow from the Father – a new mindset, and an angel to come to teach you and awaken you.

These angels will do this to any who seek and desire, but often it is the presence of fear on any level that hinders the awareness of angels.

Fear may appear like a dimensional thing – not necessarily a demon or a principality, but like a belief that something that seems insurmountable. Demons will often put you into a moment of trauma or a moment of a scare. They will use a scare tactic to get your soul to align with fear in agreement that you never want to do that again. That is one of the bigger blocks and it is in your soul. Perhaps it was a horror movie that brought about the occasion where fear came in. Repent for exposing yourself to that movie and ask the Father's forgiveness. Then ask Him to restore anything that was stolen from you because of your surrender to fear.

The more you step into your spirit and the more you live from your spirit, the more conversing and engaging with angels is the most natural thing to do. To converse with angels, sense their presence, and harmonize with the frequency of angels cannot be done from your soul. Your soul does not have the capacity to understand the frequency of the angels. You must be living from your spirit to understand and to be in that dimensional, spiritual frequency to resonate with your angel. Therefore, the scripture says to worship in spirit and truth. The frequency to engage with your angel operates via truth, not deception, and operates within the spirit arena, not the souls' arena.

Worship Opens Portals

Worship opens portals where angels come frequently. They love to be around worship because they cannot wait to worship. **The frequency for this is called focus**, whereas a saint focuses to worship Jesus, or to worship the Father. The soul holds the desire, and the natural thought comes to begin to worship, but as you do, you are meant to press through to your spirit and allow your spirit to come forth. That switch is like morphing. Then, when you are *in spirit* and you worship, your discernment is heightened and that is when you will know the presence of angels. Since angels operate on frequency, when the right one, such as in my wife Adina's music,[10] is being released and your spirit agrees with that frequency, your discernment or awareness harmonizes with the angels that have come.

Donna had another question for Ezekiel. "When you have no fear but you recognize a need to speak to your angel, can you describe how that works and what it's like when you do it wrong and when you do it right?"

When you do it wrong, you act like a toddler throwing a tantrum when they want a toy that their parent has put away. You want something immediately. For instance, you see something that is unjust, or you have a moment of panic, and in that moment, you are operating from your soul and scream out for what you need. Acting out of that soul frequency does not help you at all. It does not achieve anything, but sometimes people act from that side of themselves. That is where you need to quiet your soul, press into your spirit, and call your spirit forward. (See the footnote in Chapter 7 under Mind Mapping.)

---

[10] Adina Horner's music is available at www.adinasmelodies.com

Moving from Soul to Spirit

From the spirit, a spirit filled believer first harmonizes with Holy Spirit to know what to do, then you can begin to cooperate with your spirit. It is the practice of moving from soul to spirit that quickens your spirit person with faster, more frequent, and easier co-laboring conversation, as well as regularity of engagement with angels. Moving from the spirit is always better than moving from the soul. This is the mark of maturity of a child of God becoming a son of God.

Donna remarked, "Recently I have been taking notice of the things that really are very soulish and gratify my soul, and I have been wondering why I have been doing this."

"It is linked to a memory," Ezekiel replied, "There are some things that you have associated with a good memory and your soul finds it pleasing. What you are really doing is noticing the barrier or the place where soul and spirit can interact, but you can behave soulishly or you can be in the spirit; you can choose in that moment."

"One of the reasons I have been doing that and not knowing it is because I have been determining where the boundary is between my soul and my spirit. Because I have practiced being in my spirit more, that practice helps and will help me discern the realms of Heaven and help me determine the presence of angels," Donna explained. That is what growing up in the spiritual realms is all about.

"Have you sensed the barrier against that?" Ezekiel asked.

"Absolutely!" she replied. "It is that barrier arising from your soul, which is nothing but your soul stomping on your spirit. You can and must take authority over your own soul."

Going a little deeper in this engagement with Ezekiel, Donna asked, "When I recognize that my soul is stomping on my spirit, what is my door to my spirit?"

"Recognition of the goodness of the Father, gratefulness, thankfulness, intent, and desire help you step over into your spirit," Ezekiel explained. "It is related to frequency. It is harder to step into your spirit when the frequency in your atmosphere is saturated with the natural realm."

Donna explained that Ezekiel was giving an example of when she speaks to someone who is talking from their logical brain and is analyzing facts. Donna would rather pursue the answer from the spirit but sometimes feels blocked. The reason for the blockage is because her friend had made an agreement to be in the soul only. Doing so affects the frequency of the atmosphere, which causes a person who wants to be spiritual, who wants to step into their spirit or wants to operate from their spirit, to struggle with doing so. It is more difficult, though not impossible. He went on to explain that often, you must come away from that environment and change the atmosphere where you are. Donna likes to turn on Adina's music, and she has a diffuser because she sometimes needs to change the smell of the atmosphere. That is what going to a "secret place" in your closet is all about.

Many intercessors are getting exceptionally good at this and appreciate the secret place closet and the ease for prayer and worship they find in that place because it is akin to a portal or pathway to Heaven.

Chapter 9
How to Work with Your Angel
Part 2

As we continued learning how to work with your angel, more understandings were given to better enable and strengthen that engagement.

The Power of Agreement

Working in the spirit realm pertains to ones' level of agreement to allow their spirit to engage with Holy Spirit. If fear is present, one cannot work in the spirit realm effectively. The fear will limit you. Your agreement comes from your spirit, which must speak to your soul and say, 'No, we are going to do this." The soul will step down, and with practice you will be able to press through the veil. When you are operating from your spirit, you harmonize frequencies with your angel. Your angel knows immediately when you have done that.

Each person must learn what their trigger for engaging with Heaven and the realm of the spirit is. It seems to be somewhat unique to the person. That is the point of seeking. To seek what works for you is a sign of hunger and maturing as a saint.

Always seek what works for you.

When people are together with you, you have set the atmosphere, and you have the portal open through a sound frequency and by inviting angels, you have made it easy for people to experience Heaven.

"Why would you not just teach them that they need to do that on their own?" Ezekiel asked. "It is all of these things: setting the atmosphere by finding the frequency of Heaven and inviting the angels to come near will create an ease of accessing Heaven."

I give you permission to test out what works better for you.

The Stance and the Sound

For some, what works to engage with Heaven and the realm of the spirit is a specific physical and spiritual stance. For others, the physical stance of stepping into the realms of Heaven blocks them. With some people, it is the sound, and for still others, it is the knowledge of what it would be like to be taught by angels, the knowledge that they are soul and spirit and *they are able to be what and how the Father created them, with the ability to be spiritual.*

Many are captured under religious training that has shut the door to their spirit side, mainly due to fear. Much fear has been taught out of pulpits and preaching. The enemy has a heyday with this because anyone who has learned fear will be fearful, and when you seek fear, that is what you get.

Anyone who has been taught fear will be fearful.

Do not Cooperate with Fear

One of my instructions related to Heaven down is to teach people not to seek fear. You must understand that **you cannot agree with fear and seek the Kingdom of Light at the same time.** It will *not* work. Your soul will overrule your spirit because of that belief system.

When teaching people how to step into Heaven, I tell them that junk (demonic encounters, etc.) is not invited to the party. Because it is not invited, I have never had to deal with any. The reason is that I have my focus pointed toward Heaven, not toward the supernatural arena in general. For you, it will be determined by where your focus is pointed. Let me remind you to look or do an internal check – where are you directing your focus?

People often do not realize where their focus is. They do not realize they have the innate ability from the Father to point their focus toward fear or faith, to darkness or light. Most people have not been taught about focusing intentionally.

Bloodline Beliefs

Ezekiel continued to explain that another thing at work which must be dealt with is bloodline beliefs. He gave a few examples to help us understand.

Mockery

One thing that shuts down the ability to engage with angels in a bloodline is mockery. This can manifest as mockery of the Holy Spirit, mockery of the Kingdom, mockery of the realms of the spirit, mockery of the blessings of God, or mockery of the names of God – in short, mockery in nearly any form.

Mockery creates a blockage or a hindrance. Some may not know that this exists as an iniquity of their bloodline. Mockery that is multi-generational is certainly an iniquitous pattern in many families. If you recognize it in your family, you must repent for it.

How do I know if it is in my life? Ask yourself, "Have I ever mocked Benny Hinn, Oral Roberts, or Kathryn Kuhlman? Have I mocked the late D. James Kennedy, Billy Graham, Franklin Graham, or other evangelists or ministers? Is mockery of the supernatural a habitual issue in my family line? If the answer to any of these questions is yes, you have an iniquity in your bloodline, of mockery. If I see a healing take place, do I mock it or doubt its validity? Any time I mock, I am placing myself in a position of judgement over the validity of something. Since you and I may do a poor job of judging correctly, we should leave that to the Father – the Just Judge.

The Church since its infancy has mocked the spiritual side of things. The adversary made them feel it is either fairy tale, it is weird, or it does not make sense to the soul, so they mock it.

You must repent for agreeing with the spirit of mockery and for any mockery in your own life, whether wittingly or unwittingly. You must also repent for carrying around the attitude that "I am going to look at this, but I might mock it," which is a form of judgment. I am going to reserve **the right to mock this**. The Church in its early days did that quite a lot. Therefore, it is in a lot of bloodlines.

Most of you reading this book are likely in the "charismatic" camp. Perhaps, prior to your embrace of this form of belief, you may have mocked those "holy rollers," or "tongue talkers," or "mystics." If so, repentance may be in order.

Like any generational bloodline cleansing, we seek the blood of Jesus to cleanse the bloodline by purification of the mocking. We must deal with this because a spirit of mocking exists that seeks to corrupt bloodlines and hinder them from experiencing the supernatural arena. We need to repent of the mocking and forgive, bless, and release those who introduced it into the family line, and do the same for all who perpetuated it throughout the generations. We must also repent of our own mockery. Then, ask for a cleansing of all the impact and ramifications of the mockery, and release blessing to those who were mocked. Request restoration of your ability to cooperate with Heaven that was affected by the mockery in your bloodline.

Fear

Fear, which we have already discussed, can also be a generational iniquity. If you recognize it, repent, and ask the blood of Jesus to cleanse you and your bloodline. **You must deal with fear in the bloodline as well as mockery.** Just as generational mocking must be repented of, you also need to request to be made sensitive that you do not agree with mocking or fear in the future.

Shutting Down Spiritual Sensitivity

Many parents need to repent where they have shut down the spiritual knowings (or sensitivity) of small children. Often, this is demonstrated in the imaginative growth of their child or where the child has had a dalliance with imagination that is actually linked to the Holy Spirit (and not an evil or demonic spirit) because small children are very spiritual. They are incredibly open, like a little open gate. They often have no preconceived fear. Most fears are instilled by the parent. Parents' descriptions of the "boogey man" and similar things often instilled unnecessary fear in their children.

Parents often put a boundary line on their child's imagination and on the spirit realm as it pertains to their child. That must be repented for in the bloodline as well because it is possible your parents did it to you. They may have taught you to be afraid of angels and other appearances.

This is not to say that a parent would intentionally shut this down in a child. More often, it is because the parent does not have a grid for the operations of the spirit in their own life, much less in the life of their child. Or the parent does not want to deal with it because *they* have a fear of it, so they shut it down in the child without even knowing it at times.

Some shut down the use of the imagination for cultural reasons. They want their child to be "normal." For a child with an active imagination and who talks with angels, that may be considered odd and abnormal. It is the fear of man on the parent that makes them shut the child's imagination down. Generations have been captured by false boundary lines due to parents doing this.

The antidote to that is the parents learning to trust in God. The parents must learn to trust in the goodness of the Father. A parents' trust and subsequent disagreement with the belief that this is something to be feared is vital. When humanity begins to understand that this sensitivity of children to spiritual things is a pathway to the Father from a very young age, it will change our understanding of everything from evangelism, to salvation, to operating from spirit first and soul second.

---

*Imagine a generation
with no fear in their spirit.*

This is possible in our era, and this is what our enemy is most afraid of and wants to close off.

Activating the Pure Flow of the Spirit

The pure flow of the spirit that one is born with must be activated. Some people teach that when you are born, your spirit is not awake, but your spirit **is** awake and has been since the moment of conception. It is just not activated, practiced, utilized, or addressed.

Learn to step into Heaven on a regular basis. People *need* to step into Heaven. It is a good practice and people need to be reminded how busy Heaven is. They need to be reminded that the activity level that Heaven operates from is instantaneous. Heaven always wants to relate to them and to communicate, talk, and assist them in the 3-D realm.

Many more spiritual beings than we know want to be engaged. Heaven has unlimited availability and desires to communicate with you, so build an expectation for when you step into heavenly realms. Expect to receive *from* Heaven and expect to communicate *with* Heaven.

You need to experience the flowers, the trees, and the sentient beings in Heaven. Once you have stepped into Heaven, you have stepped through the veil. This is the reason Jesus opened the veil of the Temple – to create clear access to the presence of God. The veil of the Temple blocked access to the Ark of the Covenant to all but a few individuals throughout history. Once Jesus surrendered his spirit the veil of the Temple was rent from top to bottom.[11]

Therefore, religion was never going to cut it. Heaven has always been about relationship and reality – and that is a dimensional word.

Limitless Expectation

"Do you remember when you recognized one day that you saw a limit in your life where you thought you could only call out to the Father, and you wondered why you had not been calling out to Jesus too? Then, after a period, you came into an understanding of Holy Spirit and you then wondered why you had never called out to Holy Spirit. It dawned on you that you had not communicated with the Godhead – the Trinity," Ezekiel inquired of Donna.

He answered his own question by saying, "It is because you were taught the expectation that it was limited to you, that the Father was not interested even in speaking to you, but only that you would speak to Him.

---

[11] Matthew 27:51, Mark 15:38, Luke 23:45

That comes from mindsets that people learned early on. Re-teaching is necessary, the practice of accessing Heaven is necessary, and the engagement of angels is necessary. Fear is simply the big stumbling block."

Activating Your Spirit Eyes

Many people are trying to engage with their angel using their natural eyeball rather than concentrating on their spiritual sight.

Often, people are trying to see something like a movie with their natural eyes in the 3-D realm. It is not that seeing spiritually is that different, but it *is* a different set of eyes that are used to see in the spirit realm. It is your spirits eyes rather than your body's eyes.

When it comes to seeing in the spirit, sometimes you see only an outline, especially when you are just beginning, and you simply do not see much. However, you have to keep looking.

*The more you look,
the more you will see!*

The more you focus, and the more you slow down with the intent to see, the more details you will see. Seeing and hearing work in tandem. That is another thing people do not understand. **Some need to know that their hearing can trigger their seeing and some need to understand their seeing can trigger their hearing.**

Why would you just use one sense when you are meant to use them all? You can even blow people's minds by saying, "Use your sense of spiritual smell. It is a sense. It all works together. Just like with your physical body, your natural senses all work together. Most people's natural senses work together more than they know to interpret the natural realm. It is the same thing; only you are using all your spiritual senses to interpret the realm of the spirit.

We have discussed your sight and hearing, but have you ever felt heat in your hands when you laid hands on someone? If so, that was a manifestation of Heaven through physical touch.

Have you ever smelled a wonderful fragrance that had no natural source? You were experiencing Heaven manifesting through smell.

Yes, you can even taste to discern. For example, have you ever shared Communion and the wine or juice you were consuming seemed very different from what you knew it to be naturally? That may have been Heaven infusing your time of Communion with a supernatural event.

Ezekiel the Old Testament prophet had multi-sensory visionary encounters. He could see, hear, touch, and smell the elements in the visions he experienced. You can experience the same type of thing! Expect it!

This is a very uncommon area of discussion. There is teaching and there is discussion – two different things.

Teaching is good, but then you need to have discussion. You must have time for questions. You also must have time for processing the information. That is where you are. All this seems to come from where you are focused.

Donna was reminded of a time when she was taught about spiritual smell and she went through a period where she was focused on what she was smelling in the spirit. Because she was focused on the sense of smell, she could smell more.

When you pick up a pair of binoculars, you do so with the intent of focusing on something far away you cannot see well without assistance. Put on your spiritual binoculars to look and focus.

Have you ever looked through binoculars and found they are not focused on what you are looking for or you have not found it in the sight? Everything is blurry and you are not sure where or how far away the object is. You must focus for a minute to find the object you are looking for. This is remarkably similar.

Donna and I follow the same procedure when accessing the Business Complex. When we step into the heavenly realms, we look for the Help Desk. We can see the things we are looking for because we are focused on finding them.

Donna went on to describe how she grew in this ability.

I stepped in with seeking and I allowed it to be presented. As she allowed it to be presented, it was.

"When you step in and you want to meet with me, what do you do?" Ezekiel asked.

"I step in, I ask for you. I wait, then I focus to look. I look around. I may ask, "Where are you?" until I see you.

"Today I saw you come around the corner into the lobby area because I was looking for you," Donna commented.

"That is desire. That is seeking. That is waiting," Ezekiel replied.

"Remember when the Father told you about the Cotton Candy Dream," Ezekiel asked Donna?

"Yes," she replied, and then she began to unfold the story of the Cotton Candy Dream that she uses to teach people how to step into spiritual realms. One of the nuances of the dream was about to how be a child. You need to be a child in the presence of complete acceptance, goodness, and unconditional love, where everything was good and nothing negative existed. That is how small children believe. That is what little kids come into the earth realm with. However, over time they lose that ability.

One day the Lord said to Donna, "I want to talk to you about the cotton candy dream." Donna did not know what he was talking about, so over the course of four or five days, he gave her an understanding of what blocks vision in the heavenly realm. In the natural realm we often experience an inability to engage childlikeness easily.

He said, "Think of the product you call cotton candy. Cotton candy is something that you get only at certain places, but every time you get it, or every time a child gets it, it is in a fun atmosphere. You get it at a park, festival, fair, carnival, or a ballpark. There is nothing good nutritionally in cotton candy. There is not one speck of vitamins or minerals, only calories and a lot of food coloring. Imagine that a small child sees this pink cotton candy and says, 'Oh, I want that.' It looks so good. It looks as if it would feel wonderful. It is unusual. There is excitement because it is special, but the parent always says no."

He continued, "Then, one day the parent says 'yes', and the child cannot believe they finally have access to this cotton candy."

The Father asked, "Why would the parents say yes?"

Donna explained, "I don't know, why would the parent say yes because there is no inherent good in cotton candy?"

He said, "Just because it was the hope and dream of the child."

It is the dream that adults miss. That is what shuts down creativity and vision for the future in the natural realm.

Imagine that you are the child who wants the cotton candy and your parent says yes. You can have as much cotton candy as you want. On top of that, imagine that this cotton candy has no negatives attached to it. It is just cotton candy and you get to have as much as you want. That could unlock something in an adult because they have lost the ability to think like that. It has been shut down.

> *You judge your answer before you have even dreamed your dream.*

Donna shared this story with a lady who was a breast cancer survivor. She is James Nesbit's (the prophetic artist) wife, Coleen. Apparently, sharing the Cotton Candy Dream really touched her because the next day James sent Donna a graphic[12] and he said, "You need to use this graphic when you talk about that because it was meaningful to Coleen. She did not realize she had shut down seeing in her life."

---

[12] More beautiful artwork available at www.jamesnesbit.com

The Father instructed Donna to use that dream to help people understand how to step into the spirit realm. This brings the freedom to **just be childlike** and not worry about anything but this wonderful ability to have cotton candy with no negatives.

This story could be a key to helping people realize their self-given limits or self-given parameters, where they see the defenses they erected and said, "I will never cross that." Many people have put up fences they do not even realize exist until they hear a story like "The Cotton Candy Dream," and they realize they have limited themselves. This could help them see these fences and knock them down. If you realize you have a fence, do a prophetic act of pushing down that fence and walking into that next place.

Ezekiel explained that a hunger exists for this. People do want to do this. Part of that is because it is a function of the realization that, "It is time for this. It is time for the Bride to walk into this. It is time for her to become known for this. It is time for her to be brave about this and it is time for the walls of religion to fall."

Helping Your Angel

Just because you have an angel does not mean that angel always has all he needs to work on your behalf. Angels have needs, and you can learn to be sensitive to those needs and keep him or her functioning at maximum capacity.

How to Arm Them Up

On a very regular basis, we will ask our angel to come near and ask him if he needs anything. Sometimes he lets us know he is fine, while at other times he will have specific requests for us. When angels have needs arising from their service to us, we must make the requests of the Father on their behalf. They cannot do it themselves. This ensures a co-laboring between humans and the angelic realm.

For instance, Ezekiel has, on occasion, requested more arrows, so we petition the Father for arrows for Ezekiel, the ministry angel for LifeSpring International Ministries, and his ranks. (He has charge over other angels who assist him). It is as simple as that. Some of the things we have been asked to request are as follows:

- Arrows
- Bow & Arrows
- Swift Bows
- Crossbow
- Fiery Arrows
- Fiery Darts
- Fiery Rocks
- Fireballs
- Fire Pebbles – goes into crevasses where darkness is hiding and lights it up
- Explosives in a pouch
- Slingshots (aka Goliath Killers)
- Axe
- Sledgehammer

- Spears
- Short swords
- Scintars – small swords
- Scimitars – large curved swords
- Swords
- Broadswords
- Shields
- Ropes
- Lassoes
- Binding Instruments
- Chains
- Smoke
- Smoke Screen – provides concealment in a battle situation
- Flail – spiked ball connected by a chain to a wooden handle. Used to go around the shield of an enemy combatant.
- Weapons for hand-to-hand combat
- New armor
- Hourglass
- Encircling – an incendiary object
- Backup – sometimes they need more angels to assist them in their work, particularly when in battle
- More firepower – at times more weaponry is needed, but not necessarily more angels.
- Frequency bombs
- Dragnets
- Nets – useful for the capture of exceedingly small entities

- Bird Nets
- Chaos Nets
- Harpoons
- Battering Ram
- Scrolls
- Maps
- Map of the new season
- Astral maps
- Underground maps
- Bars
- Undoing – a frequency weapon, particularly for witchcraft induced frequencies in people, time, and places. Enables angels to shut portals
- Expansion of Ranks
- Booby traps – incendiary devices that will explode or capture an enemy by surprise
- Quietening – enables the quietening of atmospheres where conflict is abounding
- Angel Elixir (or Tonic Elixir) – like an energy drink for angels. It refreshes and brightens them.
- Angel Bread
- Angel Food – translates to comradery among angelic ranks
- Permission to pursue the enemy raiding parties who have been sent to plunder realms
- Scribe Angels

In the preceding list, we gave explanation as we knew it where we thought it helpful. The purpose of many of the aforementioned items can be ascertained, yet some items we do not understand at this time.

One of the best ways we can assist our angels in their work for us is to pray in the spirit. Paul gave hints to the power of praying in tongues in 1 Corinthians 14, where he taught on the subject. In verse 8 Paul refers to a trumpet. That word seems out of place, but it was a marker pointing you to Number 10:9, where the trumpet is described as a means of directing the troops in battle. A purpose of speaking in tongues is to direct angelic troops in battle.

Tongues also builds a framework for revelation to abide in, so build your framework large. Do you want a utility shed or a warehouse? Speak in tongues accordingly.

Speaking in tongues does more than you are aware of, as your angels hearken to your words and flow with it in dimensional spaces that speaking in tongues creates. It is as though when we speak in tongues, it creates pathways in the spirit realm for our angels to traverse through so they can get where they need to go to faster. You might describe it as a worm hole.

Speaking in tongues enables the angels and is a way of co-partnering with them in taking care of issues that arise. Paul further instructed us to not forbid the speaking with tongues,[13] and these are just some of the reasons why.

This chapter was from a teaching by Dr. Ron Horner and Donna Neeper at our Heaven Down 1.0 Conference. The video is available for purchase from

www.courtsofheaven.net/shop

---

[13] 1 Corinthians 14:39

Chapter 10
Capturing Your Dreams

Donna Neeper shared in our conference on Capturing Your Dreams. The following is a transcript of what she shared:

It is going to feel a little bit like switching gears in the spirit because we have been talking about seeing and seeing issues on land. I want to talk to you about night season dreams, so take a big breath and say, "Lord, I'm ready to receive what the angels have brought or the Holy spirit is here to instruct regarding my night's season with you. Thank you, Father."

This morning I awoke with this topic on my mind and had no idea Ron would ask me to minister on it.

How many of you, by raised hand, are dreaming one to two times a week? Now keep your hands up. If you dream every night, raise your hand. If you do not dream nightly put your hand down. If you dream about every night lift your hand. You did not see this, but almost everybody put their hand down and only four were left with the dreaming every night.

Your spirit is alive in the night season and awake. Your consciousness is sleeping so that your body can recover your soul and so your body can recover in the night season.

The nights are highly active for your spirit man. Your spirit man is sometimes getting an understanding of where your spirit goes. Some of us are beginning to learn that we can ask our spirit to go do a thing while our consciousness and our soul is asleep, and some of those things are going to come to you in the form of dreams, because your spirit is going to be either in an activity, or it's going to be receiving a download in Heaven, and it is going to translate to your soul what looks like a dream.

So, you awaken in the middle of the night, turn over and go, "Whoa. I was in Africa, slaying snakes," or whatever. That is in my previous teaching,[14] to write that dream down and do not let it go. Dreams are very much like a vapor, and you think, "Oh, I'll remember this. How could I ever forget this?" Then two hours later, you are like, "Wait, what was that? Oh, I wish I had written that down." How many times have you said that?

You are meant to dream, but this is my point for right now, *the enemy is stealing your dreams from you*. This is how it usually happens. I am going to give you a scenario

---

[14] Donna taught more on this subject in our Business Conference 1.0. Videos are available.

and a part of a picture from my life when I was about eight.

At that age I was terrified to go to sleep at night because I kept having the same dream – the same dream over and over. I would go to sleep and I would dream that I was on a deserted island. I was all alone except for a tribal witch doctor wearing a mask and his regalia and he was chasing me. I had no way off the island, and I would run around being chased, trying to hide from this wicked witch doctor.

Every time, at the end of the dream, I would see a bridge and I would think to myself, 'Oh, I can get off the deserted island by taking the bridge.' I would go take the bridge and as I ran up to it, I realized it was only half a bridge. I had no exit.

Now, I am really stuck because if I go forward, I fall off the bridge. If I go backward, I must deal with the witch doctor.

Remember, at this time I am only eight years old. I had this dream numerous nights in a row and somewhere along the line I said out loud, 'I don't want to dream.' Guess what happened? I did not dream, and I did not dream for a long time – decades.

When I was spirit-filled in my early forties, I had been spirit filled for about a week and I had the most epic dream! It was epic. I could tell it to you right now. It was that vivid. It was one of those epic dreams, and it was the Lord speaking to me. I realized later it was to help awaken the dream state in me because part of my calling and my assignment on the planet is to help the body of Christ dream and to learn to interpret their dreams.

Do you see the connection of why the enemy would come with a wicked nightmare to an eight-year-old who doesn't even know that she's going to say, 'I don't want to dream. I don't want to dream tonight.'

It is interesting to me that I never said, 'I don't want to go to sleep.' I did not say that. What did I say? 'I do not want to dream,' giving the enemy legal right to shut that avenue of visual communication completely down for most of my life. Then, God reawakened it and it just took off.

Some of you are being stolen from because you may have done the same thing. Think back if you were a dreamer in your younger years and try to recall when the dreaming stopped. Chances are that around that same time something was going on that you wittingly or unwittingly said something that shut your dream communication down. Does that resonate with anybody?

Let us just do a group repentance because we want that ability back. It is a particularly important communication pathway of the Holy Spirit with your human spirit, with the Father and with Jesus. You may have experienced great disappointment regarding a dream, and you shut down your dreaming ability. The repentance can apply in both directions.

We are going to stand before the Father in the Mercy Court.

Just Judge, we ask permission to enter your Mercy Court today in the name of Jesus. As we enter in, we ask you, Father, to hear our repentance.

Say this after me:

Father, whether I knew it or did not know it, I did it. I repent for saying that I did not want to dream. I repent for coming into agreement with not wanting to dream. Whether I did it by fear or ignorance, I ask you to forgive me. I repent because now I see what I did. I see what happened. I ask you to restore, in the name of Jesus, for my night seasons, all my communication pathways, both visual and hearing, by the power of your spirit in Jesus' name. Amen.

Now Father, I just asked that angel you showed me this morning, the fiery angel to come. I ask that sir, would you come, and would you minister? Would you reawaken the night season dreaming?

An angel is here. He has a vial of firewater. Here we go. Thank you, Father. Thank you. In Jesus' name, I reawaken – I reactivate – the dreaming season in the night.

Repeat after me:

Because of this court work, I hereby call my night seasons sanctified unto the Lord and holy unto Him.

I will receive by the unction of the Holy Spirit and no other spirit will I receive. Amen.

Sometimes in our spiritual maturing, during the process we find ourselves coming out of some mixture into a purer stream. That is the essence of maturity, isn't it? In that process, we can have what we are absolutely a hundred percent convinced and know in our knower that that was the Word of God. We can know that we saw something. Know that we knew it absolutely by his power. It was not in the 3-D realm. It came from Yahweh. We can know that.

Often, what happens to us is our flesh steps in because we are growing up in Him. During that time, we may have a powerful encounter and we take that event and we began putting the 3-D realm lens on it. Then, it begins to shut down the pathway because Yahweh gives those visions because he wants them to expand, but he needs them to expand with angelic help and with the help of Holy Spirit through dreams and visions and through confirming words from the body of Christ.

What can often happen is that we will be willing but because we are three-part beings;[15] our soul, having not

---

[15] We are a spirit, with a soul that lives in a body.

been told its place, wants to have a say. So, it will insist on having input and you will err a little bit as we are learning Holy Spirit's leading in this realm. It happens to all of us and there's grace for it, but it does happen. What we need to do is lean over into the soul arena and now our soul is having a lot of input. Our soul can hear confirmations of prophetic words and confirmations of visions, right?

What this does, though, is prevent you from seeing the next sign. It is where we miss the signposts on the road on the journey of the vision coming to pass. It is then that the enemy is most wicked and wounds us. He blinds us and then we do not see the next sign.

Some of us never were taught that if you have a vision, you need to look for the next sign, because if you have one sign, another sign is going to come and you'll see it. Pause to wait on the Lord and ask Him to show you the next sign. You do not have to make a move. You are a child of God. I do not *have* to do anything. He will make it happen. You can simply say, "Papa, I'm available. Show me that next step (again, if necessary)."

Sometimes we forget that next step – that next sign that we need to be looking for. Your soul is going, "I'm really, really impatient. This is taking too long."

So, what happens is our soul will get excited because the vision or dream electrifies the soul to make a movement in the 3-D realm, because your soul is connected to this 3-D realm. So, the dream or vision (or prophetic word) will fire up your soul and say, "Okay, I have that vision. I am going to do this and now I am going to move there or do this thing." Your soul is ready to "help" your spirit out because it wants to have activity in the 3-D realm.

You may have had portions of your life where you feel as if you have a vision. It was absolutely and completely down your alley. Yet you may have erred because you did not allow yourself to wait on the next sign, but let your soul get all excited and lead you astray. However, the great news is we can repent.

If you feel like you have had a vision where that may have happened, or where you realized you had a vision but never saw it come to pass and it hurt you, now your soul is in a wounded state. If that has happened to you, then you need some assistance to receive healing from the Father.

Pray this with me:

Father, we ask for access to the Mercy Court. We are here to repent on behalf of our soul. Father, I repent for not waiting. I repent for not allowing you to show me the next sign, and the next, and the next. I repent for getting out of your timing. I repent for being impatient and letting my soul lead. I ask for your forgiveness and I receive your forgiveness in Jesus' name.

Father, from this repentance, I also ask your court for restitution of where I have been stolen from, due to my error that I have just repented for. I ask this in Jesus' name.

Father, I also ask of you for a healing in my soul. Make me whole as if it never were regarding that thing that I am repenting for.

Now, I receive your mercy. Thank you.

If you prayed that, realize angels are here and they have brought healing balm. Just hold your hands out and receive it.

Now the last thing I want you to do, as we are still in the Mercy Court. Look the Just Judge in the eye and say:

Papa, I forgive myself for missing it, for impatience, for ignorance, and for not knowing. I thank you that I can forgive myself because Jesus has forgiven me, and I will never look at this event in the same light anymore. Today, it changes, because I am healed and whole in You. Amen.

Chapter 11
Questions & Answers

Question: If you ever faced a situation where something once flowed in your life well, but it was eventually shut down, what were you facing?

Answer: Why would the enemy work so hard against us in our maturing to shut down what we knew, without a shadow of a doubt was a vision from Heaven? Why would he do that? Well, he's guessing, he doesn't know, He is guessing that if he can get you to agree that God is not that good and project all that negative onto the Father, then he can completely shut down every vision you were supposed to get in the next part of your life.

Let me repeat that. Satan has no prior knowledge. Satan is just doing a lot of guessing. He is watching us as the heirs, and he is trying to figure it out. "Where can I mess this up?" He is hoping to get your agreement and he will use a wicked evil mess to do that.

He would want to work overtime when he knows that you have a vision and you are all excited about it. He is watching. Satan knows you. Maybe he cannot tell exactly what you received, but he knows you received something because you are out telling your Christian friends. You are receiving confirmation words from prophets and people under the unction of the Holy Spirit, and that sort of thing. Then he watches. Then you do something and then he watches some more. You act, but nothing seems to happen, and you begin to doubt. You begin to come into agreement with doubt. Why didn't this happen? That, coupled with any wounding in your heart, is all that he needs to get you to shut down the next vision and the next vision. He cannot afford you having visions because that is a pathway of communication that is sanctified to the saint. You and I are born to have dreams and visions consistently.

We are also meant to talk about them with each other. This is our bread to talk about, to share fellowship over, and often we have it, but we have not grown up knowing what to do with it or we don't have a safe place to share it.

You do not want to share your vision with someone that is less spiritually mature than you and have them shut it down, right? We must get wise. We have to grow up in Him and we have to go, "Oh, this is my inheritance. This is the kingdom of God. Men walking in signs, wonders, and miracles will be some of the first signs." Those were visions or signposts and they are everywhere.

Understanding Your Dreams & Working with Your Angel

One of the reasons I love talking about dreams is because often dreams are prophetic, so they will come to pass. Yet there is a protocol you can learn to know when to expect the type of dream that is going to come to pass. We are not alone. Papa is constantly talking to us. He is constantly wanting to share what the angels are bringing you, what they are doing, and yes, we can step into heavenly realms. Like we have been talking about, you can get this in the night season. You can get your calendar in the night season too.

We have also been talking about your angels, knowing your angels, how to cooperate with them, and how to engage them. This is the inheritance of the saints as well. A lot of times you're going to see your angel in a dream first, before you interact with your angel from your spiritual sight, hearing, or from the natural. I also believe – and I'll be this bold – we are supposed to see them even with our natural eyeballs. They did in the Bible. We are supposed to know and discern the angelic. They are from that higher dimension and they can manifest in this dimension. It is easy for them when they choose, but what if they prefer for us to discern them with our spiritual sight and engage in that communication?

All these things, the enemy wants to steal, but the Spirit of God is here to fill you up and help you understand "This is who I am. This is who I have always been. I may not have known it at that level, but I know it today!"

Question: When you are talking about seeing with your physical eyeballs and then you shut it down because it freaked you out, how do you undo that?

Answer: We need to step into the Mercy Court and repent because you probably made an agreement concerning not seeing. Repent for making the agreement, ask the Just Judge to cancel the agreement, and ask him to restore your spiritual sight.

It is part of your gifting, and it is written in your DNA and in your scroll to see the angels of God with your natural eyeballs, just like we have been talking about.

Why would the devil cause you to fear when you saw something that your spirit was so aware of? You may have had an open door at that time in your life, so let's just repent for any agreement that would have given him the legal right to make you fear against something so sanctified and holy that was manifesting to you, because this is part of who are you are and part of what you're going to walk out.

> *Father, we step into the beauty of your Mercy Court. Thank you. In the name of Jesus, Father, we desire to repent. I agree with the adversary that I shut down this incredibly special and precious gift, Lord, that you would want to give me. I repent for coming into agreement with fear of something so beautiful and so holy and so sanctified, and something that was very commonplace, especially in the book of Acts.*

Lord, I ask you that you would forgive me, bless me, and release me, Lord, from any ungodly agreements, any impact, any agreement with fear or the adversary that shut these gifts down. Father God, I forgive, bless, and release myself, and I forgive, bless, and release all those that have impacted me in that way. I forgive even those in my own family lines that may have had the same gifting and shut them down, going back to the hand of the Father and as far forward as my descendants go.

Lord, I ask that the blood of Jesus would just wash away every impact, every consequence, every sin, and that they would be cancelled today in this court, in Jesus' name.

I receive your forgiveness now. I ask for my gifting to be activated, and every time I have been stolen from by the enemy, that the enemy would pay me back double, that I might see, taste, hear, smell, and feel what you were manifesting from Your Kingdom.

I receive it now in Jesus' name.

Chapter 12
Conclusion

As this book came to a close we were aware other revelations would follow but would be in another volume. The majority of the information in this book was from encounters specifically for the business conference we had recently conducted.

The more we engaged Heaven the more profound the sense of holiness, care, and love that the Father has bestowed on this revelation. In the weeks following the conference we have had testimony after testimony of doors unlocking for favor, provision, connections, and much more. An ease has settled upon some of the attendees who have been able to obtain their Declaration of Trade and Deed of Commerce and Trade. Some have branched out into new arenas that had not been thought of before and they are seeing the blessing of the Father on them.

As we learn the value of living Spirit First, Heaven Down we well see more and more the invasion of God into our lives and businesses. Businesses that formerly experienced struggle will find an ease settling upon their affairs. Alignments and corrections to wrong or unnecessary alignments will occur and continue to occur as Heaven helps them refine their businesses and ministries.

These concepts may not yet be second nature to us, but they are important ones to not only consider, but also to begin to implement. Many of us have spent years going in circles never being able to branch out. Heaven now wants you to soar. Do it now – begin Spirit first! Heaven Down!

Appendix A

Learning to Live Spirit First

A challenge with how we were taught about the Christian life is that everything was put off until sometime in the future. Then, we read the letters of Paul and we experienced a disconnect. Heaven, to us, was a destination, not a resource. We knew nothing about learning to live from our spirits. We only knew what we had been doing all our lives, since birth, and that is to live to satisfy our soul or our flesh. We sorely need to learn an alternative way of living.

Exchanging Your Way of Living

Paul recorded these words in his letter to the Romans:

Those who are motivated by the flesh only pursue what benefits themselves. But those who live by the impulses of the Holy Spirit are motivated to pursue spiritual realities. Romans 8:5

We must learn to live spirit first! We must exchange our way of living. We must learn to live from our spirit. We need to understand the hierarchy within us:

- We are a spirit
- We possess a soul
- We live in body

Each component has a specific purpose in our lives. Our spirit is the interface with the supernatural realm. It is designed for interfacing with Heaven & the Kingdom realm. Your spirit has been in existence in your body since your conception. Your soul has a different purpose. It communicates to your intellect and your physical body what your spirit has obtained from Heaven. It is the interfaces with your body. Your body houses the two components and will follow the dictates of whichever component is dominating,

Most of us have never been taught about having our spirit dominate. Rather, we have merely assumed that our soul being dominant was the required mode of operation.

Our soul always wants to be in charge. Our soul is susceptible to carnal or fleshly desires, lusts, and behaviors. It will, at times, resist our spirit and body. It must be made to submit to your spirit by an act of your will.

Your will is a means of instructing either component (spirit, soul, or body) what to do. Your soul has a will and so does your spirit. You choose who dominates!

Your body, on the other hand, has appetites that will control you in subjection to your soul. They become partners in crime – remember that second piece of chocolate cake it wanted? Your body will try (along with your soul) to dictate your behavior. It will likely resist the spirit's domination of your life. However, it will obey your spirit's domination if instructed, and your body can aid your spirit if trained to do so.

The typical expression that operates in most peoples' lives is that their soul is first, body second, and their spirit is somewhere in the distance in last place.

In some people, especially those very conscious of their physical fitness or physical appearance, there is a different line up. Their body is their first priority, the soul second, and again their spirit is the lowest priority.

Heaven's desire for us is vastly different. Heaven desires that we live spirit first, soul second, and body third. Since we are spiritual beings, this is the optimal arrangement. For most of us, our spirit was not activated in our life in any measure until we became born again.

If, after our salvation experience, we began to pursue our relationship with the Father, then we became much more aware of our spirit and learning to live more spirit conscious. The apostle Paul wrote in his various epistles about living in the spirit or walking in the spirit. Because we are spiritual beings, our spirits cry out for a deepening of relationship with the Father. It longs for it and will try to steer you in that direction.

Our soul has certain characteristics that explain its behavior in our life. This is the briefest of lists, but I think you will get the idea. Our soul is selfish. It wants what it wants when it wants it. It can be very pouty. It can act like a small child. It is offendable and often even looks for opportunities to be offended. Our soul is also rude.

Our body has a different set of characteristics. It is inconsiderate, demanding, lazy, and self-serving. It does not want to get out of bed in the morning, for many people. In others, it wants to be fed things that are not beneficial.

However, characteristics of our spirit are hugely different. If we live out of our spirit, we will find that we are loving and prone to be gentle. We desire peace. We are considerate. We are far more contented when living out of our spirit. Also, joy will often have great expression in our lives.

Sometimes we have experienced traumas that create a situation of our soul not trusting our spirit. The soul blames the spirit for not protecting it. The irony is that typically our soul never gave place to the spirit so it could protect us. The soul places false blame on the spirit, and must be coerced to forgive the spirit, and the soul must relinquish control to the spirit. Once the soul forgives the spirit, the two components can begin to work in harmony.

If I were to flash an image of some delicious, freshly cooked donuts in front of you, what would happen? For many, their body would announce a craving for one.

What if, instead, I showed you an image of a bowl of broccoli? How many people would get excited about that? Probably not as much excitement over a bowl of broccoli would be exhibited. Which does your body prefer? The donuts or the broccoli? For the untamed soul, the donuts are likely to win out every time. Which do most kids prefer?

In any case, you can train yourself to go for the healthier option. A principle regarding this that I heard years ago is summed up like this:

> *What you feed will live –*
> *what you starve will die*

What do we want to be dominant? Our spirit, our soul, or our body? The part we feed is the part that will dominate.

For some, they feed their soul and live by the logic of their mind. Everything must be reasoned out in their mind before they will accept it. However, because our soul gains its insight from the Tree of the Knowledge of Good and Evil, it will always have faulty and limited understandings.

How do we change this soul dominant or body dominant pattern? We instruct our soul to back up and we call our spirit to come forward. Some people may need to physically stand up and speak to your soul and say, "Soul, back up," and as they say those words, take a physical step backward. Then, speak to their spirit out loud and say, "Spirit, come forward." As you speak those words, take a physical step forward. This prophetic act helps trigger a shift within them.

Live spirit first!

Benefits of Living Spirit First

Why would you want to live spirit first? Let me present several reasons to you. Living spirit first will create in you an increased awareness of Heaven and the realms of Heaven. It will create a deeper comprehension of the presence of Holy Spirit, and of angels and men and women in white linen. You will be able to better hear the voice of Heaven. You will experience greater creativity, productivity, hope, and peace. You will become more aware of the needs of people that you can meet.

As you live spirit first, you will be able to access the riches of Heaven in your life. As a business owner, you will be able to engage more fully with the Business Complex of Heaven, and you will live a more fulfilling life. Petty things that formerly bothered you will dissipate in importance or impact in your life. You will be able to move ahead, not concerning yourself with the petty, mundane, or unproductive things that have affected your life before you began to live spirit first.

. This way of life is more than a game changer – for the believer, it is the only way to live. You will face challenges as you build your business from Heaven down, but you will more readily be able to access the solutions of Heaven as you live with an awareness of the richness of Heaven and all it provides that is available to you as a son or daughter of the Lord Most High. I encourage you, do not live soul dominated. *Live spirit first!*

Four Keys to Hearing God's Voice

Dr. Mark Virkler has written extensively on this subject over the years. It is his signature teaching and has helped thousands of believers learn to hear and record what Heaven is saying to them on an ongoing basis. His website (cwgministries.org) has a myriad of materials to assist you in learning to do spirit-led journaling. I will simply summarize his teaching here because it is a vital discipline for you to learn to maximize Heaven down in your life.

1. **Quiet yourself** – Learn to quiet yourself so you can tune into Heaven.
2. **Look unto Jesus** – we are not looking for anyone outside of Heaven to be speaking to us – they are not invited to the party!
3. **Tune to the Flow of the Spirit Within** – The Holy Spirit flows through our spirit like a river. We can learn to tune to that flow and hear what Heaven is saying.
4. **Write it down!** Begin to record what you are hearing or perceiving. YOU can judge it when you are finished listening for Heaven. Do not concern yourself with how it looks on the page.

Simply record it – whether handwritten, drawn, or typed, make a record of it!

At CourtsNet.com you will find our video course to help you in this process

Appendix B

Creating Your Declaration of Trade

Receiving Heaven's Authorization to Do Business

Establish Your Boundaries:

Stake Your Claim and define your market or audience so you can stake your claim.

The Declaration of Trade establishes your right to conduct business according to Kingdom guidelines.

Establish Headship:

Dedication to the LORD is first

Your business truly becomes a Kingdom enterprise by your dedication to the LORD of Hosts. You are entering into a partnership with Heaven to conduct your business.

He is first, you are second.

Establish the Pattern:

Agree to trade according to Heaven's principles

Your agreement is to trade according to the principles of the Father, such as righteousness, justice, fairness, weights and balances, and property rights, as well as the principle of knowing and staying in your boundaries and the principle of knowing your sphere.

Receive the Resources:

Heaven's resources await release for you

Once your Declaration of Trade is approved, your angel(s) are released to your business, as well as your accounts being established in the Finance, Creative & Personnel Departments.

Appendix C

Glossary

Alms – It is the Father's heart for the poor and the release of kindness toward others. It is gifts given to those in need of what you have received. It can be monetary in nature or non-monetary.

Angels – Heavenly beings created by God to assist the work of the Father throughout the universe.

Author's Symposium – A resource of the Business Complex of Heaven focused on anyone who writes as their occupation, part of their work duties, or part of their scroll.

Business Complex of Heaven – A major resource center in the realms of Heaven geared toward business, creation, development, and management. It consists of several departments.

Business Crisis Center – As a resource of the Business Complex, this center wants to help one's business. Whether one is in crisis or going into a crisis, Heaven has resources and strategies whereby the business can come through the crisis into a place of wholeness.

Business Recreation Department – As one of the departments in the Business Complex of Heaven, this department focuses on the recreation needs of employers, employees, and the customers or clients of the enterprise.

Cloud of Witnesses – Consists of saints who have passed from earthly existence into eternity in Heaven. It contains the Men and Women in White Linen, the 24 Elders, Patriarchs, and others. Each believer has a cloud of witnesses working on their behalf from the realms of Heaven.

Creative Department – One of several departments in the Business Complex of Heaven. This department contains resources to unlock creativity in individuals and businesses for the furtherance of the Kingdom of God upon the earth.

Declaration of Trade – The foundational document of any enterprise, granting the recipient the authorization of Heaven and a trading floor in Heaven from which to conduct business.

Deed of Commerce & Trade – The actual title for the trading floor for a business or enterprise. It is coupled with the Declaration of Trade.

Dimension – a concept difficult for our minds to understand but a dimension is composed of realms and realms are composed of territories.

Division of Motor Vehicles – One of the departments in the Business Complex of Heaven. This department contains resources to aid in the transportation needs of enterprises.

Enterprise – The term used in this book to refer to any business or ministry entity.

Finance Department – A major component of the Business Complex. This department contains resources related to finance and maintains accounting regarding any business enterprise.

First fruits – For individuals, this is typically a financial gift given at the beginning of the new moon to any Kingdom enterprise. It is a gift given in advance of the month out of expectation of the goodness of the Father to provide the thing(s) desired and pronounced over the first fruit gift. In business scenarios, it can be a gift in advance with the expectation of a particular benefit to the giver.

Hall of Fame – Similar to a museum upon the earth, this resource focuses on those persons who successfully learned or engaged some of the processes of the Business Complex of Heaven while upon the earth.

Heaven Down – the business building paradigm taught in *Building Your Business from Heaven Down* and *Building Your Business from Heaven Down 2.0*. It focuses on the primacy of accessing Heaven for wisdom in building one's business.

Help Desk – the "go to" place in the Business Complex of Heaven. All interactions should begin here as individuals engage the Business Complex. They maintain resources and can direct you where to go regarding a business's needs.

Library – A resource of the Business Complex containing information about any subject someone might need more knowledge of.

Men in White Linen (also Women in White Linen) – Refers to saints who have passed from earthly existence, and who now serve the pleasure of the Father, working on behalf of the Father and of the saints upon the earth.

Marketing Department – As a component of the Business Complex, the Marketing Department contains resources for and can give input into any arena of marketing an enterprise may be involved in or need to be involved with.

Offering – a gift (usually monetary) given out of the thankfulness of one's heart for the blessings of God.

Personnel Department – As a component of the Business Complex, this department assists and advises concerning any employee, contractor, partner, or other similarly related aspect of an enterprise. They maintain records on each person involved in this type of relationship and can assist you in the procurement or dismissal of personnel for an enterprise.

Portal – a passageway allowing for the flow of activity from the spirit world into the earth or other locale (or vice versa). Both godly portals and ungodly portals exist. Godly portals facilitate the angelic and heavenly access to other realms, while ungodly portals provide for access of the demonic and ungodly into other realms. Godly portals were often referred to as whirlwinds in the Bible.

Realm – a place of existence. Any living entity is a realm. They may be composed of any number of realms within themselves. Realms are composed of territories and realms (with their corresponding territories) are what makes up realms. Cities are realms, nations are realms. Saints are designed to have dominion over realms.

Steward – one who performs the duties of caretaking. This can be over a territory or realms.

Storehouses - refers to the wealth of Heaven's available resources and contains the sense of invitation to the saints in Jesus who are able to draw from that dimensional realm: wealth, healing, Heavenly encounters, revelation scrolls, and every needed resource.

Strategy Room – Where you can go in the Business Complex to obtain Heaven's strategy for any aspect of an enterprise.

Tithe – a tenth of ones' income designated for holy purposes. From an individual, a tithe was originally designed to be given to ones' local storehouse (house).

Travel Agency Department – If it is travel related, this department of the Business Complex can assist you.

Everything from advice to smoothing the process of the travel itself can be obtained in this department.

Business Advocate Services

www.basglobal.net

BAS exists to help business owners, entrepreneurs, and ministry leaders learn to engage Heaven first in building their enterprise. We help businesses build from the top down rather than from the ground up. This distinction is vital to powerful, accelerated growth so you can maximize the strategies we unveil.

Our Services

Corporate Training

Is your business stuck? We can coach, advise, and train your staff to maximize the strategies from the Heaven Down business building style and help get your business unstuck.

Business Conferences

BAS provides training in the Heaven Down paradigm for business building. We can customize events for your type of business, i.e. real estate/property development, online marketing, etc.

Corporate Consulting

We provide ongoing consultant services to help you stay on track with your marketing plan and strategies. We can provide monthly, quarterly, and semi-annual check-ups to keep you on track.

Strategic Development

Allow our experts to help you develop your business's strategic style. We can help design a working plan in line with the Heaven Down model to grow your business.

Trained Advocates

We have trained business advocates that you can employ as corporate intercessors & corporate spiritual advisors to keep your business and personnel on track.

Private Consulting

BAS also provides personal advocate services to help you stay on track with the Heaven Down paradigm. If you want to get your personal or work life unstuck, we can help." You may also contract with us to assist in implementing the concepts in this book.

Why Choose Us?

Experience: Our team is the developer of the "Heaven Down" paradigm for business development and expansion strategies. We know how to access the available information and help you implement it for your business.

Dependability: When we make a commitment to you, we endeavor, to the best of our ability, to fulfill that commitment. If we are unable to do something, we will be straight with you. By the same token, we expect the same from you.

Commitment: We are committed to your success, utilizing the "Heaven Down" paradigm for business. We work with you as thoroughly as allowed to maximize the strategies uncovered for your business.

Compassion: Although often not equated with successful business development, compassion puts you in strong connection with the source of the Heaven Down paradigm.

Heaven Down Solutions for Your Business or Non-Profit

Businesses

Businesses of any flavor can benefit from the concepts of the Heaven Down paradigm. Whether service related, technology based, or anything else, you need this information.

Non-profits

Non-profits and ministries need to be diligent with excellence to survive in today's climate. The Heaven Down model can help you truly accelerate your organization to be all it can be.

Arts & Media

The Heaven Down model is especially geared to those in the arts and media arena. We have worked with screenwriters and producers to free up creativity in their personal and corporate settings. We can help you as well.

Education

Learning how to thrive, not merely survive, in today's economy is essential for those in the education arena. Let us help you discover potential roadblocks and clogs in your institution so you can make the impact you desire to your marketplace.

Real Estate/Land & Property Development

Knowing what properties to invest in or stay away from is essential. The Heaven Down approach seeks out the potentially problematic areas in real estate issues so you can have maximum profit and growth in your projects. We stand ready to help.

Retail Sector

Whether brick and mortar or internet-based, you want your business to succeed. Let us help you discover the hindrances to your business success and help you move forward in business and in life.

Ready to find out more?

We would be pleased to schedule a private consultation with you to discuss what we offer and how we might help you. Visit our scheduling link on our website to schedule your private consultation.

Contact us today!

Business Advocate Services
Post Office Box 2167
Albemarle, NC 28002

Tel. (980) 221-1827

Email. info@basglobal.net

HOW DO YOU KNOW IF YOU NEED A BUSINESS ADVOCACY SESSION?

HOW DO YOU KNOW IF YOU'RE READY FOR A BUSINESS ADVOCACY SESSION?

- Do you already have a business?
- Do you want a business?
- Is your business experiencing blockage, stagnation, and cycles of lack?
- Does your business prosper in one season and almost die panting on the floor in the next?
- Do you have personnel issues?
- Are you ready to launch a new product within a current business?
- Do you lack vision or has your vision become stagnated where you have forgotten why you are in business in the first place?

Consider the answers to these questions and your willingness to seek counsel from Heaven regarding the principle of the Father's prosperity and preparation for those operating in new seasons of business, the sons of God.

Please note: Your willingness to change your thinking will equate in a direct measure to the result and rate of success you have from heavenly realms.

BusinessAdvocateServices.com – our business and ministry consulting extension for the Heaven Down paradigm for business and ministry growth.

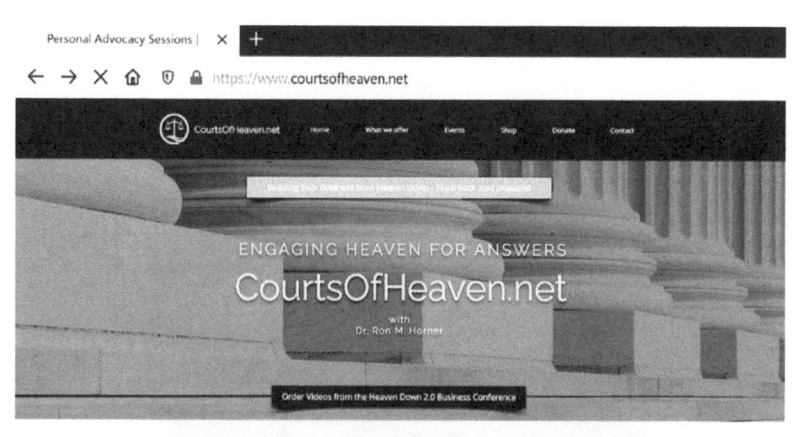

CourtsOfHeaven.net – our primary website to introduce you to the Courts of Heaven prayer paradigm and the products and resources of Dr. Ron M. Horner. You can schedule a Personal Advocacy Session here.

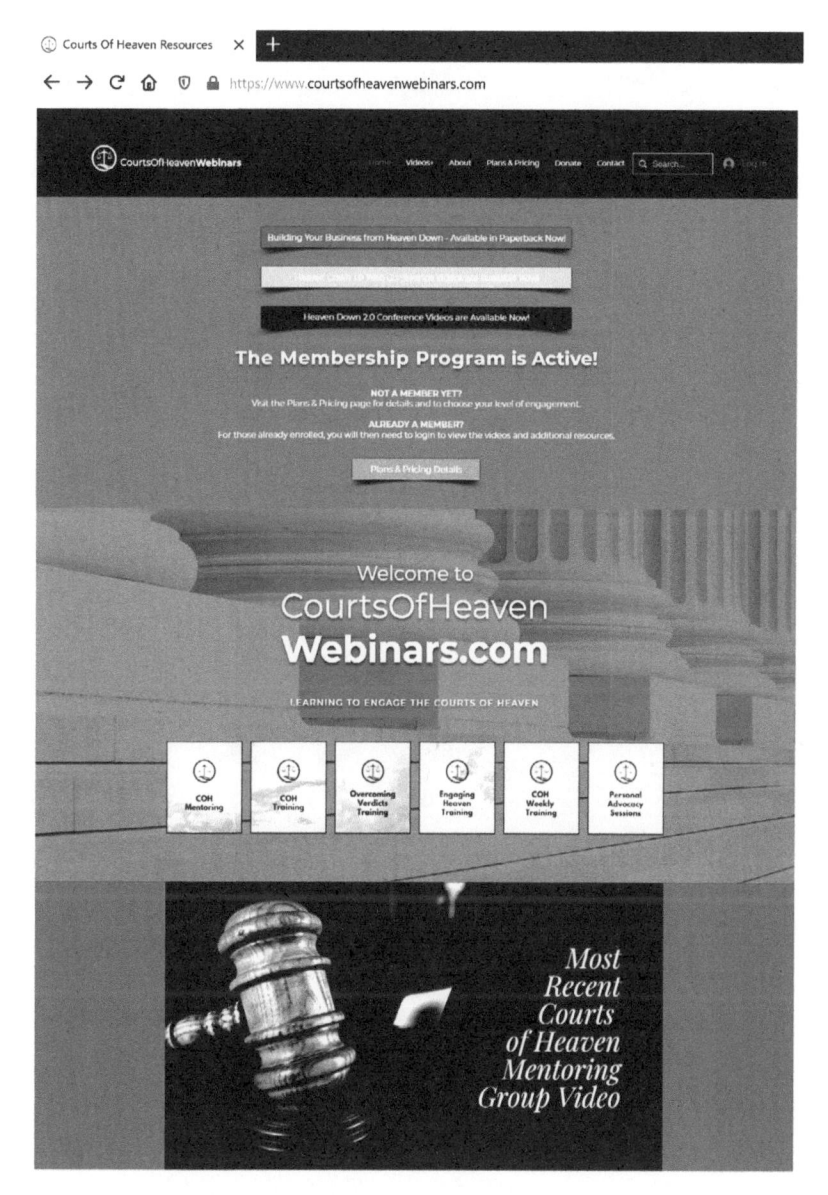

CourtsOfHeavenWebinar.com – contains our weekly training classes open to anyone as well as archives of material on the Courts of Heaven, engaging Heaven, and much more.

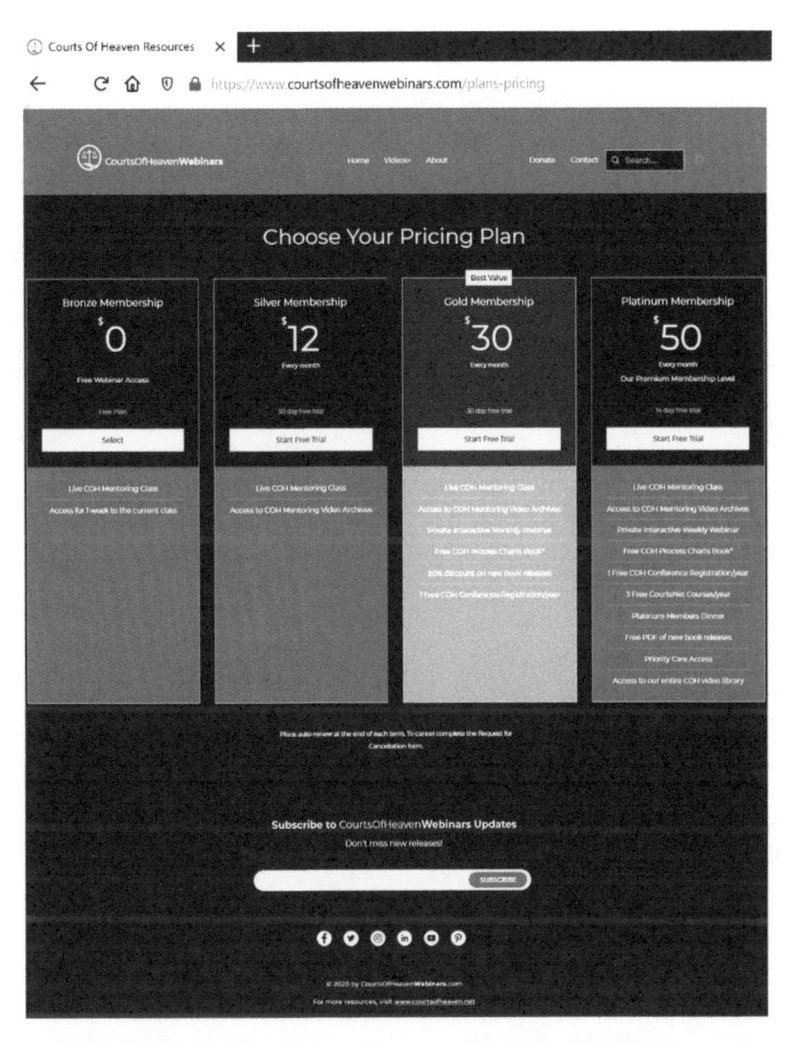

Choose your level of engagement with our ministry on the CourtsOfHeavenWebinar.com site.

CourtsNet.com – has video training on a variety of subjects including our Facilitator Training Program.

AdinasMelodies.com – contains albums for download of prophetic worship to help you engage Heaven.

Description

The realm of Heaven contains for businesses, business leaders, and business owners a deep well of revelation regarding their activity on earth in the business of their trade. This book contains more revelation regarding the Heaven Down business paradigm and helps the reader understand more foundational building blocks for engaging Heaven's release of how you conduct your business from Heaven Down. This book contains specific teaching for a business's beginning and the interesting twist regarding retroactive capabilities of these beginning steps.

Continue the journey of the Heaven Down business paradigm by reading the recent revelation as the journey continues.

About the Author

Dr. Ron Horner is a communicator and author of the bestselling book, *Building Your Business from Heaven Down: How to Receive Heaven's Input for Your Business*. He writes and teaches on this subject as well as about overcoming other life-limiters. Dr. Horner spent many years in the IT industry and has owned several businesses throughout his career. His work has taken him around the globe.

Ron is the author of over a dozen books on the Courts of Heaven and founder of LifeSpring International Ministries, which serves to advocate for individuals and businesses in the Courts of Heaven. He is also founder of Business Advocate Services, a worldwide consulting company (BASGlobal.net).

Books by Dr. Ron M. Horner

Building Your Business from Heaven Down

Engaging the Mercy Court of Heaven

Four Keys to Dismantling Accusations

Engaging the Courts of Heaven

Engaging the Help Desk of the Courts of Heaven

Engaging the Courts for Ownership & Order

Engaging the Courts of Healing & the Healing Garden

Engaging the Courts for Your City *(Paperback, Leader's Guide & Workbook)*

Releasing Bonds from the Courts of Heaven

The Courts of Heaven Process Charts

Overcoming Verdicts from the Courts of Hell

Overcoming the False Verdicts of Freemasonry

Unlocking Spiritual Seeing

Cooperating with The Glory

Lingering Human Spirits

Let's Get it Right!